FIND YOUR FINANCIAL FREEDOM

FIND YOUR
FINANCIAL
FREEDOM

Let Go of Fear, Gain Control,
& Achieve Lifelong Wealth

LOGAN RANKIN

LIONCREST
PUBLISHING

FIND YOUR FINANCIAL FREEDOM
Let Go of Fear, Gain Control, & Achieve Lifelong Wealth

ISBN   978-1-5445-2643-0   *Hardcover*
       978-1-5445-2641-6   *Paperback*
       978-1-5445-2642-3   *Ebook*

The vision for your life comes from within you. Then it is a choice whether to set out on the journey.

Along the way to Financial Freedom and other milestones, the kind of life you live is dependent on your willingness to change, adapt, and evolve to become someone capable of continuous discovery.

CONTENTS

Introduction   **ix**

Chapter 1. Should Money Stay Still?   **1**

Chapter 2. Intensity of Vision   **15**

Chapter 3. Run Your Life Like a CEO   **43**

Chapter 4. The Scoreboard   **63**

Chapter 5. Your Money Should Move   **89**

Chapter 6. Scale   **123**

Chapter 7. Legacy   **141**

Bonus—Chapter 8. Real Estate   **155**

Conclusion: Tap into the Greatness Inside of You   **187**

About the Author   **195**

INTRODUCTION

Chewing my third peanut butter and jelly sandwich of the week—and it was only a Tuesday—I wondered if our plan to achieve Financial Freedom was really worth it. But my wife said exactly what was needed to get me over those limiting thoughts: "Logan, at least we have a ramen dinner to look forward to tonight!" I chuckled and even started to look forward to those ninety-nine-cent ramen noodle cups that awaited us.

For years, my wife and I ate PB&Js and ramen noodles 80 percent of the time. We were in $40,000 of debt, mostly from student loans. Even though we were in the six-month interest-free grace period, I *feared* that debt. Ultimately the anxiety relating to the debt was what began our journey; we were eating so many noodles because we were on a budget. We'd set a goal of Financial Freedom. We had envisioned what our future life could be like and we had laid out the sacrifices it would take to reach our goal by a certain date. Our intensity levels were high because we wanted to be in more control of our lives sooner, with more options, more freedom.

It was still early in the game, though. We didn't know at the time that we would soon get out of debt, begin real estate investing, and eventually build up to 1,500 units before I turned thirty-five. The way I look at it, there's a simple three-step process that brought us to Financial Freedom and beyond.

1. Set a vision for your life.
2. Through awareness and sacrifice, organize your life to increase cash flow with your time.
3. Invest your money in assets that increase your cash flow.

We had set a vision and established our intensity level, but we weren't yet using our cash flow budget effectively nor were we looking at our net worth as a scoreboard to make each asset and liability of our net worth as *productive* as possible. At that point, you aren't only working hard for your money, but you're making your money work hard for you.

Why hadn't we made progress? Partly it was a matter of literacy versus application. I was beginning to understand the concepts, but applying logic to what you read and making different decisions takes practice. With practice, you get more feedback. And you get better.

At the time I thought all debt was bad debt. The truth is *some* debt is bad debt.

That belief worked against us despite our positive intent and drive toward Financial Freedom. We were the kids on the basketball team who put in great effort but didn't have the fundamentals of boxing out or free throws locked in. Our opponents would get the rebounds and make the clutch free throws while we couldn't get ahead. But our naive belief that all debt was bad debt wasn't the only thing holding us back.

From a young age the following was drilled into me: *Work hard. Save money. Reduce debt. Put what's left in a 401(k).* Sound familiar?

Throughout this book I'm going to share why those beliefs held me back in my teens and my early twenties, even after the milestone my wife, Ashley, and I reached in deciding to pursue our Financial Freedom together. Maybe some of those beliefs are holding you back, too.

The good news is this:

- you can go on a journey from naivete to wisdom.
- you can challenge societal norms and beliefs.
- you can set a vision for your life, put on paper when you will achieve it, and determine the intensity level at which you'll go after it.
- you can construct a cash flow budget to propel accountability.
- you can become financially literate to plug your leaks.
- you can figure out how to scale.
- you can also establish the seeds of your legacy so that your time on Earth leads to a better future for your children and others.
- and you can even learn from me about getting started in real estate.

Put a "will" or "shall" in front of the above sentences—*I will...I shall...*—and you've got daily affirmations that are the seeds of manifesting a different reality.

MY FIRST CAR

When I was sixteen years old, I bought my first car for $3,000. It felt great, because I'd been disciplined for three years. I worked and saved, worked and saved, worked and saved some more. Meanwhile, some of my friends spent their money on fun but smaller things, but I worked and saved for the bigger prize.

For a moment, put yourself back in the mindset of your sixteen-year-old self. Do you remember driving for the first time? Free of your mom and dad's supervision? In my first car it felt so good to peel off the side streets onto the open road. *Whoosh.* The freedom and the thrill. I remember thinking, *Dang, I'm glad I worked so hard and saved all this money—look at me now!*

Problem was, I totaled the car a week later.

One totaled car and $3,000 down the drain. That was a tough pill to swallow, but I didn't despair or give up. If anything, it brought me back down to Earth. Still young, the fire in me was properly lit and I knew I could accomplish big things and that I could make money to propel me on that path. After all, the money let me buy the car; the car made me feel free.

How could I make more money?

Sure, I could work some more. But I didn't want to do *only* that. Was there some other way?

To answer this question, I looked to school, I looked to friends, I looked to teachers. I even asked Mom and Dad.

But the answer society gave me was the same: Logan, continue trading your time for money. Time for money didn't seem like the best option, but in the beginning, at that young age, I couldn't yet expand my thinking to take on a different view or look inside myself for the answers. I didn't know what I didn't know. In school, we were being taught formulas and theories but not about taxes and investing. But even if we had been, there may have still been a problem: being fed facts without being given practice in how to evaluate knowledge does not give you power. Even if they'd given us a financial literacy course, we would still have needed a basic course in *logic* to interpret the knowledge we picked up in books, podcasts, and through personal experience. The lack of financial literacy and foundational logic courses means that each year more teenagers graduate from high school ill prepared to manage the flows of money that are integral to successful participation in society. It's too bad because kids really are smarter than we give them credit for. So why are we withholding the practice in applying logic and reason to all this knowledge already at their fingertips? Because most of us "adults" are ill informed and financially illiterate as well.

Reflecting on the crashed car and my reaction to that event, I see that this situation was a chance to open my mind to change. It was also a chance to embrace a childlike curiosity. By simply asking *why*, one can playfully challenge the norms and beliefs society has offered—norms that your ego may have accepted to keep you from reaching your potential. And yet, even if I had been smart enough to inhabit that beginner's mindset and look deeper than the answers society spoon-fed me, I didn't yet have the experience of being through the wringer. Direct personal experience is a valuable source of knowledge because it is untainted by culture, which introduces the filters of an influencer's agenda or outright poison in some domains.

There's also the reality of how one's environment shapes a person. Growing up as a teenager, I didn't have money, financial literacy, or wealthy family and friends. There was no one to divulge the finer details of money, investments, and taxes. I worked three jobs and drove a car without a speedometer into my midtwenties.

After college I went to work for a corporation because it was safe. They valued performance and results, and I started moving up and getting paid better. That's great; who wouldn't want promotions and more money? But beware. As Kevin O'Leary of *Shark Tank* famously said, "A salary is just the drug they give you when they want you to give up on your dreams." Now, I don't necessarily think a W-2 salary is at all bad, and I happily accepted this myself for a decade. *But*, the salary was part of my plan toward Financial Freedom, not something that I *had* to do. I chose it. Since I liked my job, I worked harder at it, receiving new responsibilities and promotions that went along with that.

These days, on the internet, you can find many books about working hard, saving, and staying disciplined, even investments. But these should be paired with a process to evaluate that information. In this book I'll share with you how I track and process the information about my basic financials. Most important of these is cash flow. The metrics I focus on are whether my assets and liabilities are generating cash flow, and how much that cash flow is changing month over month for each of those line items. Where foundational logic was the missing piece to critical thinking, I discovered cash flow to be the cornerstone of Financial Freedom.

But let's not get ahead of ourselves. You first have to decide if you want to be financially free.

LIFELONG WEALTH AND MAKING
THE CHOICE TO BE FREE

Some people believe that Financial Freedom isn't achievable, period.

Are you one of those people? Probably not. But maybe you've picked up this book because you're on the fence. You've been told that one day you could own a house. And yet, your desire to have a house does not prevent others from having a house. Many good things in life, often the most essential, are available to everyone. The Declaration of Independence says it well: "We hold these truths to be self-evident, that all men are created equal, that they are endowed by their Creator with certain unalienable Rights, that among these are Life, Liberty and the pursuit of Happiness." Money can be viewed as a kind of facilitator of a better life, which enhances your liberties and pursuits. Money isn't required to have moral courage, to tell the truth, to act with integrity, to work on yourself spiritually. Those things are intrinsically meaningful pursuits that this book won't focus on. But if you *didn't* have those, would you even want Financial Freedom?

This book is going to focus on removing the unnecessary stresses of money, finances, and investments from your life, and beyond that unlock the options available once you've achieved the milestone of Financial Freedom. Through practice you will make mistakes, learn, and grow—just as working through difficult emotional traumas frees you from those energy-absorbing abysses. At the end of the day, it is money being put to work, not your time being put to work, that eventually buys you your freedom.

And everyone can be free.

When I began reading about Financial Freedom and learning the truth, I made a decision. I sat down with my wife and showed her what I'd learned. She understood it. Just like you can watch an online tutorial from a complete stranger to help you change a light bulb or an entire light fixture (even if that tutorial is really just a commercial), you can, with only a little effort, grasp the fundamentals of money, cash flow, and investments. With practice, your decision-making (which is really just applying logic to that knowledge) will improve and you will start to see results.

That day my wife and I made a joint decision. We would reach Financial Freedom by age forty-five. Remember: you must *choose* to be free. That commitment starts a chain reaction. Through planning, discipline, and sacrifice-based decision-making, we got there much sooner than we imagined: *at thirty*. That's fifteen years *sooner* than we thought! And much, much sooner than society would have advised. Obviously, I'm glad we didn't wait to get started, because we're enjoying the freedom-giving benefits of Financial Freedom sooner than we ever imagined. We are new, better versions of ourselves. But also, being fifteen years off goes to show how much I didn't know, how much society had influenced us, and how fast you can learn if you ask the right questions.

Have you been putting off your Financial Freedom? Don't let it get you down if you made mistakes, since mistakes are natural to the learning process. Don't be discouraged if you have procrastinated until now. Let go of that negative guilt: sometimes those who procrastinate are on the verge of a life-changing pivot. You're here. You are even here for a reason. Read on.

After taking the journey, I learned that self-education was critical. Having the belief in myself, the confidence that I could learn and also discern what was useful, empowered me. Now I want to share the principles of achieving Financial Freedom with anyone who is waking up to the truth that Financial Freedom is possible not only for others, but for them too.

How did my wife and I achieve Financial Freedom by age thirty, a mere seven years into our journey? As I share lessons throughout this book, I'll also tell that story. It was not without losses and mistakes. And even recently, after a decade in real estate investing, I bought a property where the tenants owned the AC units but where I was under the impression the property did—a $20,000 mistake.

In this journey, my wife and I learned to communicate to each other what we wanted, we learned how to make a cash flow budget, we learned how to evaluate the investments, and we figured out how to make our money very productive to better light up our scoreboard. Most people are taught how to work hard for money. **But they aren't taught how to make their money work hard for _them_, too.**

We started this journey toward Financial Freedom when we invested in our first single-family home in 2013, and it left us with $7 in the bank. That year I underwrote the property—a financial analysis to inform me of the benefits, risks, and the debt. That showed me the cash flow would be $3,400 in year one. On $20,000 down to purchase the house, that $3,400 in revenue represented a 17 percent Cash-on-Cash (ConC) return. Now in reality we only made $3,200 that year on that property, or a 16 percent return. I was actually quite happy to see that come out close to my forecast, a contrast to my lack of crystal ball skills in the stock market. It's better to focus on what you understand already or are capable of understanding with enough study and discipline. From this perspective, the true impact wasn't really the returns. It was the control and understanding. Any fear of the unknown decreases with increased understanding. As for control, up until then I hadn't been taught and didn't expect to have control over my investments. For example, ask yourself: After one year, how much money will my 401(k) produce and with what confidence can I forecast that? Did that return show up in your bank account?

By contrast, with real estate, I had control. We kept investing in real estate and learned how to get better returns on that investment. It was a grind early on because I didn't have the money to invest heavily nor the education. I learned later that the education is even more important than the money.

It took three years to reach just seven units. By the end of year four, we had seventeen units. By year five, we added fifty, for a total of sixty-seven. As of 2022, we own over 1,500 units and more than $150 million in real estate. These days whenever I think about spending a dollar, I still hesitate because I know that spending it doesn't give me a return, but investing that dollar will.

WHO THIS BOOK IS FOR

When I started to wonder about what I'd downloaded from society about money, finances, and investments, it led me on a journey to not only get out of $40,000 in debt, but to build a real estate investment design and implementation plan that would lead to my family's Financial Freedom. It meant recognizing that the program I'd downloaded from society wasn't optimal. What would happen if I downloaded an updated program? Better yet, what might happen if I threw out the software package completely? What would come to pass if I activated my creativity and wrote my own story? This would mean reverting to my intuition, skills, and perception, and putting them into practice.

This isn't a guide to get rich or get rich quick. It's important to be thankful for everything you have at each stage in your journey. What I'm sharing worked for me, yes, and on a relatively short time scale—seven years to Financial Freedom from age twenty-three to thirty—but I'm not focused on dollar amounts as a first principle. You can be financially free living a humble, frugal lifestyle. At the same time, if you want to live in abundance, that is up to you as well. As you start to stack money, you'll have the option to decline or give into lifestyle creep— where you spend a little more than you were before—and enjoy a few more comforts than you did while in the trenches of your path to Financial Freedom. But that choice is yours.

I'm also not here to offer a formulaic approach about spending habits or the power of compound interest, which makes me cringe when I hear it now because it is very slow when compared with my approach, which velocitizes money. Instead, in these pages I'll share the power of an actionable process applied to a vision of Financial Freedom. Any of the most successful ideas in this book I've compiled either from other books or from direct experience. I'm striving to tell stories and explain things in a way that has resonated with me and for my students, mentees, and attendees at workshops.

I've shared who this book isn't for. What about who it *is* for?

This book is for those who are looking for a different path in life that will allow them to allocate time toward leaving a lasting legacy, no matter what life stage you're in. Maybe you're a teenager: here's your chance to get a great foundation in these pages. Maybe you're like my wife and I were, in our early twenties, in our first career jobs. Or maybe you are in your forties or fifties or sixties. Even then, there is plenty of life ahead. My mom and dad invested in their first real estate at age fifty-eight and only two years later they retired a full five years ahead of their expectation. Even if up until now you've listened to or resorted to society's default options, you'll see that you can retire sooner and make your money work harder for you from now on.

This book is foremost for those ready to challenge themselves. To challenge your expectations of what you can accomplish. To challenge your own beliefs. To challenge yourself to step up to the next version of yourself.

This book is for you if you're ready to confront the lies you've been told, or that you've told yourself, about money, finances, and investment. It's also for you if you're eager to learn how to make your money reach its full potential and work as hard as you do.

But we won't stop there.

This is about building a mindset, understanding, and blueprint to achieve the kind of Financial Freedom you desire. Financial Freedom is a destination for some, but just the turning of the page into a new chapter of life for others. To help you take one step at a time, I'll walk you through my approach to the cash flow budget, net worth reviews, and how I scaled my real estate business. You don't need an MBA to learn any of this. Whether you're blue collar, white collar, or no collar, all are welcome. This will take hard work. This will take sacrifice. But I promise, you will leave this book feeling fired up, armed with the tools and confidence to make impactful change in your life *today*.

I'm not one to tell you what to do, but if I may be direct, I recommend putting whatever comes into your consciousness into action as soon as possible. If that means putting the book down at times so you can update your cash flow budget or setting it aside to take action on a new income stream, so be it and more power to you! If that happens, the ROI from the purchase of this book will probably be stronger than most other investments you've ever made. If for the cost of this book you get started on a new path, that will be more than worth it for both you and me.

FINDING *YOUR* FINANCIAL FREEDOM, YOUR WAY

In *The Matrix*, Morpheus tells Neo, "I can only show you the door. You're the one that has to walk through it." This can happen at any time for someone at any age. What matters more is your preparedness for the consequences of that decision and your willingness to go through any perceived or actual hardship once you do.

With that in mind, there are a few ways to read this book:

1. Cover to cover. I recommend this strategy for those who want Financial Freedom really badly. Read every detail. By taking a patient, disciplined approach, you will gradually learn and practice lines of questioning to go to battle with the inhibiting ideas, habits, and routines in your life beginning with Chapter 1: Should Money Stay Still?, Chapter 2: Intensity of Vision, and Chapter 3: Run Your Life Like a CEO.

2. Want to learn what underpins my overall approach to money, finance, and investments? It starts with a three-step process in Chapters 2–4 where you'll set a vision for your life, build a cash flow budget, and finally, make your money work hard for you.

3. Back to basics. In Chapter 5: Your Money Should Move, I answer questions posed in Chapter 1 about saving, debt, and investments. You may end up cashing out your 401(k) as soon as possible, so don't say I didn't warn you.

4. Need help on choosing your investments over the long term? Start with Chapter 3: Run Your Life Like a CEO, proceed to Chapter 4: The Scoreboard, and finish with Chapter 6: Scale.

5. Want to leave a legacy? Give your sons and daughters activities to practice building financial skills in Chapter 7: Legacy.

6. Looking for a primer on real estate investing? Jump to Chapter 8: Real Estate, this book's bonus chapter. I'll walk you through my story and process to finding my Financial Freedom through real estate investing, including the reason why I once spent $20,000 when I only had $20,007 in the bank, or the time I chose to ride my bike to work because my car broke down and we didn't have enough to get it fixed or buy another.

WHO YOU WILL BECOME

Have you faced setbacks? Where have they put you? Maybe you are in deeper debt than I was. Maybe you no longer believe in yourself. Maybe your spouse has lost trust in your ideas about money management. But before we go any further, understand this: if you are willing to understand money, you will learn how to make it productive. If you are willing to make a cash flow budget, you will learn how to evaluate your decisions and how you spend your time, bringing increased awareness to your life generally.

I've done a cash flow budget alongside my wife for more than ten years. Set aside laziness and convenience. Like any good routine, through practice we've learned about money, investments, and ourselves. We went in thinking this routine was merely about Financial Freedom, but the vision for our partnership and for our family has exceeded even our lofty early expectations beyond monetary considerations alone.

I spent the first decade of my professional working career working for a Fortune 50 corporation where I led retail operations and moved up quickly through various leadership positions building high-performing teams and managing large P&L portfolios. During that time, I was able to lead and implement strategic operational changes at the enterprise level across the US. When you are working for someone else, you are helping them become profitable. When you are working on you or your investments, you are directly impacting *your* situation. Through hard work, a systems approach, and a huge push for a growth mindset, we were able to achieve Financial Freedom by thirty.

I've built two multimillion-dollar businesses. The first is a real estate investment business, which I own and operate with over 150 different properties and more than 1,500 total units, valued at over $150 million. (Important to note: I own this 100 percent and this was not done with syndication or partners.) The second business I've been able to build from the ground up is my property management business, which now has over 50 employees and eight digits in revenue. This business focuses on managing both my properties and my employees' properties. I won't get too in-depth, but we have large goals in this company to not only improve people's lives in all levels but also to disrupt property management altogether.

Two other businesses round out my responsibilities. One is a coaching business where I get to teach what I know to new and intermediate-level real estate investors, to make it possible for them to get into real estate themselves and also to scale. I've helped more than two hundred people who either didn't have real estate investments or had a few to ramp up their game. Then there is the hard-money lending business, which essentially loans money to real estate investors so they can get started and grow or scale faster if they don't have money, and also helps to move my money faster.

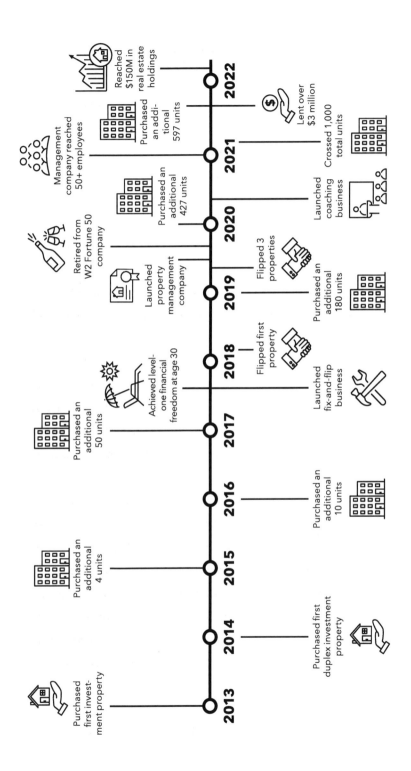

2013 — Purchased first investment property

2014 — Purchased first duplex investment property

2015 — Purchased an additional 4 units

2016 — Purchased an additional 10 units

2017 — Purchased an additional 50 units; Achieved level-one financial freedom at age 30

2018 — Launched fix-and-flip business; Flipped first property

2019 — Launched property management company; Flipped 3 properties; Purchased an additional 180 units

2020 — Retired from W2 Fortune 50 company; Purchased an additional 427 units; Launched coaching business

2021 — Management company reached 50+ employees; Crossed 1,000 total units

2022 — Reached $150M in real estate holdings; Purchased an additional 597 units; Lent over $3 million

Finally, my wife and I are very focused on starting a foundation to help with Financial Freedom, health, and affordable housing to plant seeds for the future. In 2021, in both time and money we donated more than we had in the previous ten years combined.

Jordan B. Peterson said that "if you have something to say, silence is a sin," and that is part of the reason I'm writing this book. I have something to say about becoming not just financially secure or independent, but financially *free*. Along the way, you'd be wise to exercise your free thought, free expression, and free choice.

It really comes down to this. If you are willing to set a vision for your life and use a system to pursue it, you will learn that not only is it achievable, but it's reachable sooner than you think. If you've faced setbacks, have faith that the comeback is far better. And finally, remember: Financial Freedom isn't a destination—it's a way of being.

Imagine a future where you create your own schedule, spend time how you want, coach your kid's games, and are more present as they grow up, seeing the world. Most of all, imagine spending your time on what *you* want and not trading it for money but using money to gain that time back. Once you begin to wake up and see the dawn of this new world, you will be able to leave behind old thinking, which can be constricting, and take on a new overview, a welcoming perspective, a warm embrace of a fresh adventure. Who you become is more important than what you accomplish on this journey. If I lost everything tomorrow, I'd be able to build it all back faster than I did the first time. That knowledge is also part of the mindset and reward of Financial Freedom.

YOUR PROGRESS REPORT
TOWARD FINANCIAL FREEDOM

1. Honestly challenge norms and beliefs
   (first up!).
2. Decide what Financial Freedom is to you, when
   you want it, and with what intensity level.
3. Define and boot up the systems to run your life
   like a CEO.
4. Light up your scoreboard.
5. Become financially literate.
6. Learn how to scale.
7. Teach your sons and daughters to fish.
8. See how I built my real estate business.

The Three-Step Financial Freedom Process:
1. Set a vision for your life.
2. Through awareness and sacrifice, organize your
   life to increase cash flow with your time.
3. Invest your money in assets that increase your
   cash flow.

CHAPTER 1

SHOULD MONEY STAY STILL?

"You need to constantly challenge your own thoughts."

—SAM ZELL, REAL ESTATE INVESTOR

All these years later I can vividly remember the bowls we ate our ramen out of, how the sandwiches tasted, the gloomy feel of the apartment. But what is more distinct is the fear that I had about our debt. Even during the grace period, I didn't want those debts looming over my head. I didn't want to be stuck in debt for decades. Wanting Financial Freedom, I was nevertheless still under the spell of the scarcity mindset and neglected to notice alternative paths to my potential, financially and otherwise. I was worried about the future instead of utilizing my resources in the best possible way in the present moment.

Up to this point in my life, all I knew to do was save more, pay off my debt, and put the rest of my money in a 401(k), because that retirement account was the only thing I'd done as far as investing went. It felt secure and a mature thing to do. It's what I'd been taught to do. Was it taught to you this way as well? But I really didn't understand anything, because solely putting money in my 401(k), which is merely a tool or vehicle like any investment, should not have been the sole focus of my investment strategy. (But let's be even more clear: I didn't have a well articulated investment strategy yet.) Now, in a world where there are many social pressures, there was no social harm in not understanding my investments. Without outside pressure to change, I didn't have to change. When I'd ask around, those in my circles didn't understand their investments either. The change would later have to come from within.

The crux of the mistakes I was making at that time was this: *our money was sitting still.*

The truth is, if you want to be wealthy, if you want to grow your money, then your money cannot be idle. If your money is caught flat footed like a basketball defender who gets crossed over, the money depreciates at the hands of inflation, the invisible tax.

The prevailing mindset was if I worked harder and saved more we'd eventually remove that debt burden. And we did. We did it in only nine months. But *man*, we didn't have to do it that way. What would have happened if we'd started our real estate investing *first* instead of first paying off that grace period no-interest student loan? We'd have achieved Financial Freedom sooner. These what-if games aren't useful spiraling into but it is worthwhile to integrate lessons into future decisions. Investing in real estate before paying off my student loans—or doing both simultaneously—wasn't an option because I didn't know what I didn't know. It wasn't like we entertained real estate investing and decided against it; it wasn't even on the table—ramen noodles were.

When I compare myself then to who I am now, I'm not even the same person. You aren't the same person today who made mistakes and learned from them in the past. By simply reflecting on this truth you can move forward. I've changed and evolved. It used to be that when I made a dollar I thought about saving it or paying off my debt. Now when I get a dollar my first thought is how to invest it. I ask, How productive can I make this dollar? Or, Is there a way to velocitize it? When I invest it, how long until I get that dollar back so I can do so again? I doubt that is how many of you reading this book were taught to think, or how you naturally think today. Maybe that will change by the time you're through this book.

So, to start, in this chapter we are going to challenge basic norms or beliefs you may have about money, finance, and investments. This starts with *questions*, not answers. If answers are given too soon, you risk taking bad advice from an influencer. And even if I turn out to be less shiny and more real than others, don't fall in the trap of taking what I say as the Gospel. Because you miss out on drawing conclusions for yourself through the application of logic to data, including your own experience.

When you challenge your thoughts, you can pick the good ones, discard those that are troublesome, and otherwise learn to discern through critical thinking. Then, in Chapter 5, I'll share what I think about the questions raised here. This is your chance to think again, to look at old questions with fresh eyes. By the time you get to Chapter 5, with enough curiosity and research you'll probably already have formulated answers to the questions raised here, and it will be interesting to see how your answers and mine may differ. In that case I welcome disagreement because iron sharpens iron.

If you ever get stuck, just remember, in the most simple terms what matters is how you move your money. If it sits still, it is stagnant and more likely to collect dust and lose value. That can be fine under circumstances of high uncertainty, where holding that dry powder lets you take advantage of major unforeseen shifts. But in general, if you make your money move, if your money flows, then good things will happen.

PRECEPT #1

PENNY SAVED, PENNY EARNED

It's always been interesting to me that people are so quick to talk about how you need to "save" more to build wealth. Penny saved, penny earned. Don't spend too much, because then more can be saved. But have you ever wondered why a third option—investing—hasn't been readily shared? Or maybe you've even been told saving *is* investing? Truly think about today's world. What happens to your money as you save and save some more?

But if you're like me, you've questioned this precept in general. You've questioned whether the best option for your money is to just sit there. Does your money just sit there when you open a bank account?

Have you ever questioned what is being done with that money as it "sits" in the bank? Answer this: How do banks make their money? Are banks putting their money in the bank? Why or why not?

PRECEPT #2

DIVERSIFY YOUR INVESTMENTS

Mark Cuban, *Shark Tank* investor and owner of the Dallas Mavericks, once said, "Diversification is for idiots." In my early twenties, I didn't understand what he meant and most of my investment money was in a 401(k) spread out across a huge index of stocks. I guess I was an idiot when it came to money; this was the safe play for me at the time. I was following the traditional playbook. Is the traditional playbook still as relevant today as it once was?

The traditional way we are taught to invest is by throwing money into an investment like a 401(k) and ensuring it is diversified among many different stocks. But when it comes to the 401(k), is it *really* an investment? Or is it a tool? I'd argue that it is a tool that allows you to make investments in mutual funds, stocks, bonds, and indexes. The 401(k) was the only "investment" I knew anything about until my midtwenties and it was invested in a ton of different indexes and stocks I knew nothing about. It certainly was the investment I heard about most and was encouraged to get. I've heard it said that having money in a 401(k) is not only a great investment, but a good way to avoid spending that same money if it went into your checking account instead. But I think it's worth challenging your beliefs just a bit.

Do you have a 401(k)?

If yes, can you name where it is invested?

Do you know what you're paying for fees? (Not the percentage, the *exact* amount.)

How much control of it do you have?

Do you understand the rules and regulations? Do you even understand the places where it is being invested?

Have you ever been taught about a company match?

Not only could I not answer these questions when I started investing in my 401(k), but also it took a few years before I even asked the questions.

If you also had to look up some of these or didn't know the answers to those questions, is this really an investment or are you making a gamble based on what you've been told?

When you take a second and think, it's a bit weird to realize you haven't questioned where your hard-earned money is going. It was for me. Why didn't I know how hard it's actually working? Why don't I have more control over it? After all, it's my money that was invested, wasn't it? Why is it so hard to understand and why is it comparatively so easy to auto-draft from my checks to these investments? How many millionaires got there through a 401(k) alone? Are the people recommending you must have a 401(k) to be financially where you want? Have you ever heard of someone becoming rich because of their 401(k)?

Once I started questioning why the 401(k) was my only investment, I'll share what I decided to do. But the key learning I made was that the 401(k) was not aligning with my vision for Financial Freedom. It bothered me that my money was sitting still, that I couldn't move it without penalty, and that I was missing out on other investment opportunities because of that.

If you're eager to take action right now, you could take the above list of questions and review all your investments, one by one. What other advice are you receiving from society regarding retirement planning, products, and strategies? This will set the table in terms of your awareness relating to the return on investment each of your investments is giving you. If you are already aware, this will freshen your understanding and help you once we get to the point in the Financial Freedom process where you are looking at your cash flow budget and tracking your net worth's productivity from the standpoint of each and every asset and liability's contribution to monthly cash flow.

PRECEPT #3

FINANCIAL ADVISORS ALWAYS GIVE GREAT ADVICE

Have you ever sat down with a financial advisor and asked yourself what you hope to get out of this meeting? Given their title, maybe you are interested in financial advice, retirement, or financial planning.

Now, let me next ask you this: have you ever been more confused after the meeting than when you came in?

Here are some more simple questions to get you thinking:

As a result of working with your financial advisor, do you have a better understanding or more control of your finances?

Do you feel you fully understand the fees you are paying? Why is the fee structure so complicated? Is it fair that your financial advisor benefits regardless of whether you do?

Do you understand if they truly are helping you retire on par with your vision? Are they financially wealthy? Did their vision work?

If you are paying a financial advisor, you probably have some level of trust with them. Even if you feel great about your advisor, it's worthwhile considering that unless they are perfect, they cannot always give you great advice. And if you trust them, asking a few questions should be welcomed in a healthy relationship.

As before, we will go deeper into "the answers to the test" when we get to Chapter 5.

PRECEPT #4

ALL DEBT IS BAD DEBT

Have you considered paying off your house? If you were to do so, you wouldn't have to pay a monthly mortgage and your expenses would be considerably reduced. Maybe you've thought along the same lines regarding your car payment. My general feeling is that these ideas arise because of the society-imprinted idea that all debt is bad. Why do you hear this so often? Is it accurate? What substantiates such a sweeping claim? Is there a difference between a 20 percent credit card interest rate and a 5 percent car loan interest rate?

In Chapter 5 we'll walk through an example of paying off your house and also your car. But if you don't mind me having a bit of fun, may I present the following scenario. If you paid off your house and then lost your job, it's true that you still wouldn't have a mortgage to pay. But if you don't have money coming in, how are you going to eat? Are you going to eat your house? If you decide to pay off your house, that money is now sitting still because it is tied up in your home. Paid off, but sitting still.

There are several ways to make debt useful, which we will discuss further along. The biggest mind shift here is when assuming all debt is bad, a person is only looking at the expense side of the equation, not the potential income the debt could also yield.

WHY DOES SOCIETY TEACH THIS?

In *Killing Sacred Cows*, Garrett B. Gunderson discusses how "scarcity thinking brings out the worst in us including fear, pride, jealousy, selfishness, and adversarial competition." Society markets the scarcity mindset but we can replace it with an abundance mindset.

Why then is the scarcity mindset so heavily marketed toward you?

What is the result of the hand that society deals us? How is it that so many Americans are stuck in a lower-middle-class lifestyle, barely living above the paycheck-to-paycheck threshold?

In my view, parts of our near-term culture inheritance are poisoned with the scarcity mindset, which plays on our fear of loss, failure, and even death. That turns us away from the true American spirit of appropriate or even bold risk-taking, especially while you are young. It makes us nervous. It makes us afraid. We are waved into the casino of societal norms to gamble on our college education, our careers, our retirements, and ultimately our lives. But when you gamble, the house wins. You may feel like you're winning in the short run, but in the long run, if you're gambling, you've already lost. The alternative takes work. It takes work to learn but you *must* learn about money and investing instead of taking advice from people who aren't concerned with your vision.

Don't let your money sit still.

Now, if you jump ahead to Chapter 5, we'll talk through a few answers to the above questions, but it really comes down to this.

Educate yourself, put your money to work, let it flow, let it stack, and reinvest it again. Make it *move*. If you have no idea what I'm talking about with money moving or sitting still, that's okay, I didn't either. Read on and you'll get there.

Before you can make it move, it's important to slow down and establish your vision. This next part can make or break you, no matter how smart you are. That's good if you don't think you're that smart, because commitment allows you to overcome other shortfalls you may have. Intensity of vision trumps IQ. Let's get into it.

YOUR PROGRESS REPORT
TOWARD FINANCIAL FREEDOM

1. *Honestly challenge norms and beliefs.* ✔
2. Decide what Financial Freedom is to you, when you want it, and with what intensity level.
3. Define and boot up the systems to run your life like a CEO.
4. Light up your scoreboard.
5. Become financially literate.
6. Learn how to scale.
7. Teach your sons and daughters to fish.
8. See how I built my real estate business.

The Three-Step Financial Freedom Process:
1. Set a vision for your life.
2. Through awareness and sacrifice, organize your life to increase cash flow with your time.
3. Invest your money in assets that increase your cash flow.

CHAPTER 2

INTENSITY OF VISION

"In today's fast-changing world, it's not so much what you know anymore that counts, because often what you know is old. It is how fast you learn. That skill is priceless."

—ROBERT KIYOSAKI, INVESTOR

....

ife moves fast.

Responsibilities pile up.

Distractions seem to accumulate even faster.

Especially if you don't confront them. Or if you don't select your responsibilities carefully.

Set your house in order. Learn about yourself and your partner. Clear up the dispute with your brother. That will make the reading a little more pleasant.

Doing that prework makes the process of setting a vision smoother, without which you can't get Financial Freedom. As you set out, remember that this is *your* vision. For a long time, people have put their hard-earned money into an investment that dictated when they could retire. That is backwards. From here on out, you are going to start with your vision and then choose investments that serve that vision. If retirement is part of that vision, so much the better. But don't get stuck with seven figures in your 401(k) that prevents you from retiring at fifty because you didn't realize you couldn't pull from the 401(k) before fifty-nine and a half are without penalties (which set back your retirement as well).

The idea of retirement is to my view a remnant of a previous era, which the 401(k) plays into. Put your money away until *later*. What about the opportunities you have *today*? Shouldn't you have access to your money through regular cash flow so as to make the best decisions and take advantage of every opportunity that presents itself?

The answer to that question can be teased apart by examining another common precept.

MANY PEOPLE LIVE FOR THE WEEKEND

Which day of the week do you live for?

Some people feel trapped in their jobs and therefore trapped by this question. They know it isn't Sunday and it sure isn't Monday; the Sunday Scaries and the Monday Blues come to mind. They settle on Friday. If that is you, there's some very hard work ahead to understand how you got trapped and to confront the fears that make you feel like you can't get out.

Others will answer Friday, but not because they don't like or even love their job. Friday is a time to rest and rejuvenate and spend time with kids and family. To be thankful for everything that has been given to them. Those who enjoy their work, however, can still get a bit stuck in that routine and not have enough time to plan ahead to reach their financial goals sooner than they thought possible.

I worked for a decade in a W-2 job and working very hard there went a long way to increasing the pace at which we reached Financial Freedom. I am thankful that my company offered performance-based recognition and promotions. In my own real estate companies I am very focused on creating a culture that engages and rewards employees but also sets the tone that it is their choice to be there. I want their values and aspirations to align with the company's as well. I want them to love what they do. That passion will translate to results, which leads to a career that has them look forward to building something special every Monday.

That choice is something that many don't think about. They think, *Well, I have this income from this job and I have to keep doing it for a long time.* If the work you're doing for that employer is gratifying, meaningful, and rewarding, that is great. The next question to ask is, How does it fit into my Financial Freedom plan?

Jordan B. Peterson wrote: "If you don't own your vision, you may be a puppet of someone else's goals. Once you have a vision, you can stumble toward it. Even if you do so badly at first." This became relevant when I recently asked a mentee, "When do you want to retire?"

It was clear from his delayed response that he hadn't really thought about it. "I don't know, fifty-five?" he replied. For the moment let's leave aside debates about what it means to retire and if retirement will look the same going forward.

Why was this millennial's response fifty-five?

Was he really saying he wanted to work the next twenty-five years only to enjoy Saturdays and Sundays?

I want to be clear. If you have a job you enjoy, I am not recommending you leave that job. I still work every day. But now, I work on something that I am passionate about, something that benefits my wife, loved ones, and team. If you like your job, though, the next step is to think about how the money you are bringing in from that job can be put to use so that one day you can reach a crossroads where even that job you appreciate can be a choice. When your job is a choice—because you have the means to leave and you are financially free—you might even find that you like it even more. Work doesn't feel like work anymore because the money doesn't matter and instead it brings meaning to your life.

As you've seen, much of developing a vision starts with questions.

THREE QUESTIONS TO SET YOUR VISION

Sam Zell said that "if you don't know that you can't, then anything is possible," which speaks to a psychological truth, which is that if you start by thinking, *I can't*, or worse, by saying, "I can't," then you are doing yourself a massive disservice before you've even stepped up to the starting line. Those who think they can and those who think they can't are both probably right. Instead, plant a few seeds, tend to them, and see how they grow.

The time has come to wrestle with hard but invigorating questions.

WHAT DO YOU REALLY WANT?

What do you really want? By when? And at what intensity level? What does your spouse or significant other want, by when, and at what intensity level?

It sounds simple, but it's not. So let's write it down.

What do you want?

Allow yourself the chance to explore the following question: What would you do if you didn't have to trade your time for dollars?

Some people would actually do much of the same. They've focused their efforts, gained skills, improved their character, developed relationships, and arrived at a kind of work that brings them joy and adds value to others. Find what you love to do and you'll never work another day in your life. In that scenario, the foundation of the word *work* crumbles, giving way to play. But even in this case, wouldn't you want to have the freedom to continue working because you *want to* and not because you have to? Especially if the work that you love changes, or if the ownership changes, or your boss changes. One thing I know for certain, and you probably do too, is that things change and they can change fast.

If you can't work with that, maybe try answering what you would do if money were no object, or what wealth looks like to you, or what you would do with more freedom.

This isn't about short-term goals. This isn't about wanting a seventy-inch TV. This is about the biggest things you want.

Another way to enter this thought process is to envision your life in three to five years. Or ten to thirty years. Take a moment to dream. Is that what you want in the future or do you want something more, something different? Could you get there and be living that way sooner than what you may have unconsciously been programmed to think? This is your opportunity to sort out how to play the game of life, *your way.*

DEFINING FINANCIAL FREEDOM FOR YOURSELF

What is wealth to you? Does it relate to Financial Freedom, or is it separate from it?

Is your vision only about Financial Freedom, or about other things too? What are those?

If you set out to acquire wealth, how would you measure it? What would wealth allow you to do?

If you were wealthy, what would you do differently than you are doing right now?

If you were financially free, how would your approach to life differ?

BY WHEN?

By when will you be financially free?

Write down a year and even a month if you'd like.

It's one thing to want it, but saying *when* you want it will begin to shape your thought patterns to shrug off obstacles and notice tools immediately available to you. Robert Kiyosaki said that in life it's often not the smart, but the bold, who get ahead. Don't let your neighborhood's financial advisor invade your thoughts here. He may want you to think retirement is a long way off yet. Because the longer you invest with him, the better. But what is better for you?

When my wife, Ashley, and I asked ourselves the questions, we eventually settled on age forty-five. Let me emphasize something here. If we didn't ask this question, and if we didn't decide on forty-five, I don't know whether I would have even gotten into real estate. The question made me confront my limiting beliefs, including that everyone should work a big chunk of their life. We found forty-five because we thought that we would have kids of a certain age and even if we still liked our jobs we would at least be giving ourselves options by having attained Financial Freedom.

And once we'd decided on forty-five, any investment that didn't fit into that vision was no longer a good investment for us. Real estate became a good investment for that vision.

Remember, don't let societal norms get in the way. It's hard to escape them completely, but see if you can stretch yourself here. It's impossible to achieve Financial Freedom earlier in life if you don't actually believe it's possible, if you don't set a goal to get there, and if you don't have an ideal time frame of when you actually want it.

Once you've established by *when* you want to achieve your vision, it's time for the final, most important piece.

How intensely are you prepared to seek that vision? With what focus can you apply yourself? What sacrifices are you ready to make?

It's one thing to know what you want, even though most leave it as a vague dream. It's another to put a timeline on it.

You've now written down what you want: Financial Freedom.

This is huge because you've slowed down to focus and truly commit to your goal. Then you took it a step further even: you forgot when everyone told you to retire and you picked a timeline that was right for you. Without fear, without perhaps even quite understanding how to get there, but nonetheless, you have a timeline to reach this goal by... Now, the last piece in Step One is possible. And it's the most important: intensity level!

INTENSITY LEVEL

At this point you've written down what you want...Financial Freedom. This is a big moment because you've proven to yourself that you can slow down enough to focus, consider, and choose a vision. Then you took it a step further. You let go of what others told you about how to work and how long to work and picked your own timeline.

The last piece in Step One is possibly the most important: defining your intensity level.

Write down an intensity level from 0 to 10. Your partner should as well. This should be the number that measures how badly you really want Financial Freedom. Are you driving under the speed limit on cruise control? Then you're probably at a 2 or 3. If you're hovering around the speed limit, but still on cruise control—this is what society tells you to do—maybe you're in the 4 to 6 range. You make smart decisions and still like to go on enjoyable vacations. Above the speed limit gets you into the 7 to 10 range where you feel the sacrifices a bit more and are even more disciplined.

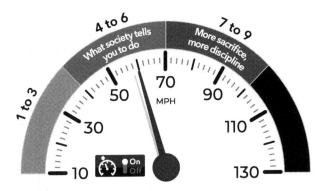

Ultimately this is a conversation about the willingness to make sacrifices in expenses and time.

Talk about what makes you have a different intensity level. Listen to your spouse and share what is on your mind. It is normal that you are both in a different spot during this assessment period; however, it is critical for you to be aligned prior to getting started. Communication and accountability through this entire process is key.

Let's say you are at a 5 but your wife is at a 9.5. My experience is that you need to meet somewhere in the middle. Otherwise your wife will be making a lot of sacrifices and you won't. Stellar communication would be required not to let subtle resentment build up when the intensity levels are so lopsided.

In my experience this conversation *has* to happen. If it doesn't, you'll probably never hit your timeline, or worse, it can be devastating for the relationship.

Probably you'll end up around a 7 in this example.

"I'm at 9; can you get to an 8?"

"No, but I think I could get to a 7 by making these sacrifices and arranging my daily routines like this."

"Okay, I think I could do a 7 as well. It will mean going a little less directly than I'd like, but I can live with that because I see you stepping up."

It's useful to really take time to listen to one another throughout this conversation. The goal is to understand where the other is coming from, what their concerns are, what they are excited about. This is a negotiation in the most uplifting sense of the word, because you are going to have to lift each other up along your journey and it's best to know how you can do that for one another from the outset. While the intensity number is important, the reason behind the number is what each of you needs to understand too.

Let's say you land on 7. Now, instead of arguing every month about how you aren't stepping up to the plate, your wife will be happier that at least you came up to a 7. Else you leave open the door to dissatisfaction or even resentment and divorce. Better to shore up the foundations at the beginning before setting out.

Remember that you've both stated you want Financial Freedom and agreed on a timeline. You have a shared vision that will anchor you. All that's left is to work through that intensity level. As you do so, you can trade a few sacrifices. What tends to happen is some of those sacrifices seem painful up front but less important as you get a few months in. You realize you didn't need some of those things. Maybe you thought some of the sacrifices weren't important but you realize those luxuries were actually essential to your well-being in a way you didn't recognize. In that case, there's an opportunity to discuss that in your monthly reviews.

A ROUTINE IS HOW YOU ACTUALLY GET THERE

I strongly recommend a routine. Tony Robbins said, "If we want to direct our lives we must take control of our consistent actions. It's not what we do once in a while that shapes our lives. But what we do consistently." Committing to a routine will help you to build the physical and mental habits that exercise your decision-making and improve your discipline. If you think you can have better results without a routine, give that a try for a few months, then come back here.

If you choose to have a routine, consider starting with a monthly sit-down. You have your cash flow budget and net worth spreadsheets and notes in front of you.

But before even looking at the financials, start by talking about how the last thirty days went. Read aloud your vision. Your timeline. Your intensity.

I want to be financially free by forty-five and my intensity level is a 7.

Do you feel that you put this goal first?

Do you feel that you focused on it?

Do you feel you made decisions the past month that align with your more important goal, Financial Freedom?

Just like people fall off diets because diets don't work, you can fall off your Financial Freedom diet if you make it simply a diet instead of making a big change in your approach to life.

You will make better decisions consciously (and unconsciously) by being honest with yourself about those three questions once a month.

If you could have made better decisions or you even made bad decisions, talk about it. That conversation alone is helpful and reinforces the practice and life change you're after.

To step back a bit, there's no excuse for the poverty trap existing *this long* in a country as wealthy as the United States of America. But, coming from a blue-collar family with little financial education, I know that reality is very different. The traps have been set. They don't have the explosive effect of, say, a land mine—but they are just as crippling long term.

Many small decisions over a long period accumulate to your benefit or detriment. This is why it is essential to slow down every month and review the decisions you made the last thirty days and truly ensure they align with your ultimate goal, timeline, and most of all...intensity level. If you didn't find perfect alignment, that's okay, you're human. Next, discuss what you'll do differently the next thirty days. Most people believe they are making sacrifices each month but really it's either you sacrifice these small meaningless things now or you are sacrificing your ultimate goal, aspirations, and dreams later. Finally, log your reflections and get ready to embrace the days ahead!

OUR STORY
SKIPPING THE MIDSIZED HOUSE

When Ashley and I got serious about Financial Freedom, we were both working full-time jobs. We liked our jobs. I was a leader in retail and she was a nurse. When we asked the question, *When do we want Financial Freedom?*, we took our time to lay it out. We had an honest discussion about what we wanted in life: being there for kids, raising a great family, controlling our time. Usually your spouse wants the same things as you do if you share a value set, though maybe not on the same timeline. Are we okay working nights and weekends? Where do you see yourself not only next year but in ten or twenty years? Then work backwards.

Maybe in a decade or so we'd still like our jobs. But we wanted options. Even with us liking our jobs, was it realistic that we would continue to like them in the future? What could change? There was the fact that both of our jobs demanded nights, weekends, and more than fifty hours a week. Again, fine now, but we asked what that looked like for kids. I wanted to coach them in sports. We wanted to spend time with them and with each other. All these considerations, and more, led us to the decision to go with age forty-five. And if we were wrong and still loved our jobs but had enough passive income to be financially free, well, we could choose to keep working our jobs but the difference is... it would be a choice.

SACRIFICE

Sometimes sacrifices can be difficult to pin down. One day it feels like a sacrifice to skip morning coffee. The next you don't feel like you even need it. To further complicate matters, when you step back and take the perspective of the long view, every choice you make is a kind of sacrifice.

To simplify things a bit, realize that sacrifices relate to a trade between having something or feeling something now and having or feeling something in the future. It's a choice between two paths. If you humbly approach decisions with an attitude of thanksgiving, that gratitude will help you make the right decision for today and tomorrow. If you ever make *what you perceive* as a mistake, be ready to forgive yourself. One action can be reversed by the next action returning you to the path you'd prefer to walk.

THE PIVOTAL QUESTION

Then we came to the pivotal question: what intensity did we have?

Mine was 9.5.

Hers was a 9.2.

Both 9s.

We *really* wanted this.

In hindsight, we were lucky. Now, helping lots of people through this process, I know if you are honest, not everyone is at the same number.

Because we wanted this so bad, we made sacrifices. There were things we gave up that we thought were important, but they ended up not being critical. A few essential luxuries will do you well, but the extra-nice things provide you marginal returns in the happiness column. Having too many things can even make you unhappy because it becomes a lot to manage if you aren't organized. I would even go so far as to say that those things you buy now that you don't need have marginal short-term happiness results compared to the long-term happiness you could have by reaching your big goals faster. Do you know how much of your income you need to live off of? Is it 20 percent? Fifty percent? As I've pointed out, lots of small decisions that happen now affect your future and most of the time people don't even realize it's happening.

Once we started our routine of talking about our road to Financial Freedom once a month, life began to change. A few years went by. Promotions came through and our family was making more money but sticking with our plan.

At one of our routine statuses, we were looking back thirty days and ahead thirty days as normal. But I could sense Ashley wanted to talk about something big. I had actually felt it coming for a few months as we heard about our friends upgrading their lifestyles. That lifestyle creep wasn't happening to us because we were a bit more disciplined and following our monthly routine.

She said, "How about we buy a moderate-sized house?"

Back then we lived in a modest $100,000 house with a solid foundation. It met our needs and was in keeping with our Financial Freedom vision and plan.

I said, "Sure, if that's something you want to do, let's talk about it. What did you have in mind?"

"Why don't we jump to a $250,000 house?"

While our house met our needs, it didn't meet our wants. And I also think as we started making a lot more money, we watched as others around us started upgrading and buying their next homes. It was becoming increasingly obvious that our monthly vision talks were proving to provide us with focus and clarity over what we wanted. It's human nature to want to upgrade in life. But examining where that desire comes from is interesting.

I didn't say No. Instead, "Let's look at our vision."

So we did. We discovered that if we upgraded, then it would likely take two years and three months longer to reach Financial Freedom. For the last few years we'd done our cash flow budget—which we'll go into detail on in the next chapter—so it was rather easy to project when we would reach Financial Freedom. In the scenario where we would go ahead and buy this house we would see a decrease in cash flow. All other things being equal, as a result of decreased monthly cash flow we'd have less money to purchase additional properties to create additional passive income. With fewer investments over time our cash flow would be lower than it otherwise would have been. We'd reach Financial Freedom slower. We did the math and it worked out to two years and three months slower. That's the power of the cash flow budget. Not only does it let you be aware of cash flow, but also allows you to predict cash flow into the future. You get better as you educate yourself and follow the process. More on that soon. For now, back to the story.

I said, "That's fine, I'm willing to compromise because we've both made sacrifices for a long time. But let me ask you first— is the new house worth more to you than those two years and three months?"

It took her less than ten seconds to say, "It's not worth it."

Ultimately our vision was not only about Financial Freedom but about what we wanted in life. And my wife and I really wanted to build our own dream house one day too. A few years later we skipped the midsized house and went from that, a $100,000 house, to a $2 million custom-built house. You might be thinking, how did they go from a $100,000 house to a $2 million one? I don't blame you. Ask yourself how many people make that kind of a jump? Almost none. Sure, you see someone go from a $200,000 to a $300,000, or a $500,000 to a $750,000, but rarely what we did. How did we accomplish that? By having a routine, by sacrificing more and longer, by making decisions others wouldn't make. We lived like others wouldn't live and now we also live like others can't live. The $2 million house did not materialize out of thin air. It came from many years of understanding our vision and making decisions every day to choose the vision of what we wanted in life versus the instant things we thought we wanted in the present.

Now, if you bought the midsized house in between, that is fine, so long as you had an honest conversation about the opportunity costs of doing so, and about what matters most to you. Communication is key.

This chapter is all about just that: taking time to have a conversation about how you are using your money and if it truly aligns with your goals. Not just your goals, but also the goals and timing of your goals. Who doesn't want a new car or a bigger house? But again, do you understand the sacrifices you are making by choosing those aims? It is not even the big decisions like upgrading your house that are the most costly; it is all the little ones like going out to eat too much, the new clothes, the expensive vacation. Opportunity cost is something rarely taught, understood, and practiced. You will see later in Chapter 6 that every dollar *not* invested on your way to Financial Freedom comes at a cost, and that cost is time.

What I've shared with you was a real conversation and that's how the conversation went.

Because we had it we were able to realize our dreams much faster, simply by revisiting our original vision in light of an alternative that presented itself. That time, the alternative would have been much slower than the route we took, simply based on having that discussion honestly. I can't stress this enough, whether it's a big decision or a bunch of small ones: revisiting your vision together and being honest about the opportunity costs associated with those decisions will make all the difference. If you want something bad enough and you are clear on that timeline, then it is easier to understand that every decision you make now with money matters.

SHARED SACRIFICE

If you have a partner, both of you need to understand and agree on the vision and goals. Truly listen to each other. This is a chance to learn and find alignment.

You both need to feel good about the sacrifices that you'll make as individuals and as a family, keeping in mind that you have to define sacrifices carefully, in case your ego is playing tricks on you.

The years of saving taught my wife and I something valuable: there are ways to have fun that are free or nearly free: drive-in movies, national parks, or camping by the lake. To this day I believe we haven't let lifestyle creep happen as much as it might have because during that period we learned how to have fun without the bells and whistles. We learned that while we may "want" something now, when we think through what we desire later, usually the longer-term goal is much better than the immediate gratification.

But finding Financial Freedom means going beyond hard work and saving. So, what are you

---

prepared to sacrifice, and for how long? Think and feel these out carefully. At your best, you will be able to choose to sacrifice the smaller, less meaningful things, the attachments and cravings and wants, instead of the long-term goals that truly matter to you.

Making these kinds of decisions now may even help later, as you get into choosing your investments.

FOCUS IS A SUPERPOWER

In today's chaotic world, focus is a superpower.

Focus lets you surgically remove distractions. Focus allows you to establish designs and plans, and to take action. Focus allows you to shoot arrows more cleanly at your target.

Practicing focus makes you even better at focusing. Because what do I really mean by focus?

Focus is both a noun and a verb.

As a noun: clarity of vision. *He has a focus.*

As a verb: the act of concentrating interest or activity on something. *He focused on the task at hand.*

Now consider a video camera. Some cameras have an autofocus feature. That's fine, except using the autofocus is kind of like saying I want society to tell me where to focus and how to spend my time and money.

Other cameras require you to manually focus.

Learning to manually focus takes practice. You not only have to select something of interest in your environment, but you then have to steady the camera, put the subject in frame, and then use your hand to rotate the lens just so to get it to focus on your chosen material.

This process will slow you down enough so that you don't get stuck focused on the wrong thing, the crutch that the autofocus culture provides you and which you may happen to accept without thinking. This is why setting up your environment, whether your room, your kitchen, your office, or your digital calendar, is critical because those settings can set your mood, update your attitude, or redirect your attention favorably.

Take time to slow down and take the time to understand what you really want. If you don't have a focus and you don't focus, you may end up living as many others do, living for only a couple days a week.

AT LEAST THIS TIME I
DIDN'T TOTAL THE CAR

I used to drive a car without a working speedometer. Since I didn't know how fast I was going I would draft off the person ahead of me. Sure, I could have had it fixed but I didn't want to waste money on that. I would have driven it longer if I could have.

One day in 2017 in the work parking lot, that car broke down. At least this time I didn't total it. Normally, I'd have gotten it fixed, or bought a new car, but we'd just purchased a few new properties. There was very little money in the bank because as fast as the money was coming in, we were stacking or saving as much of it as possible and then investing it as quickly as possible. In fact, that was my goal: make money, spend a little, save a little, and *invest it all*. Robert Kiyosaki's refrain of "broke is temporary, poor is eternal" is appropriate here. Me and my car were "broke," but I was set on not being eternally poor.

So I biked to work. For three weeks.

After many years of grinding in retail, putting in my time, seventy- to eighty-hour weeks, nights and weekends, I was finally starting to make some good money. My work colleagues may have thought I was making a sacrifice. But I didn't view it that way. I didn't care that I was first driving a car without a speedometer and then not driving a car at all, but riding my bike to work. I was making six figures at the time and cashiers at the store had nicer cars than me. And then I had no car at all. But I'd already decided. I'd already made the choice to go after Financial Freedom. I didn't want to waver, even though I could have with my salary. If I'd bought a car or taken out a loan for one, that would have been an unfavorable sacrifice because it would have delayed Financial Freedom.

For those three weeks I was nevertheless a little embarrassed to tell my coworkers about the car and my lack of funds, so I didn't, instead making up excuses about wellness. It's amazing what we will say when we are worried about superficial reputation. Meanwhile, I just rode the bike to work day after day with a smile on my face. Because we were on a mission. It was that simple. Looking back I don't know why I was embarrassed. I'm sure people would have understood if I told them that I was focused on those goals. If my colleagues didn't understand, that would be their choice, and it can take the wind out of your sails to worry what others think, anyway. Maybe it would have inspired a few people if I openly shared what I was doing then, too. Maybe it is inspiring you now? I won't be silent anymore about making sacrifices now so you don't have to make them later in life. Literally all of my money needed to be focused on assets, not liabilities. A car would not grow my net worth, so I couldn't justify it. Assets were growing my net worth. My vision and actions were aligned. I didn't have money for a car because as soon as I stacked enough money, I quickly bought another investment property. The damn car breaking down was an obstacle and the money I would have to spend buying another would mean less money on hand to buy another property. Less to invest meant to me now that my money was less productive and it also meant that as my vision became more clear, less to invest meant more time from Financial Freedom. Most don't think this way but I hope you will by the end of this book. From one perspective, everything is about time. A person makes decisions every day with their money, with their mind, and with their health that either help them buy back quality time in the future or allow precious time to slip away. Intensity of vision can change you forever. It did for us.

Take this to heart. If you can get the intensity part of setting your vision right, if you want it badly enough, you can make mistakes on what's ahead and still find your Financial Freedom successfully. When you have a committed intensity level combined with discipline and focus you'll be able to take those learnings in stride and move forward.

YOUR PROGRESS REPORT
TOWARD FINANCIAL FREEDOM

1. *Honestly challenge norms and beliefs.* ✔
2. *Decide what Financial Freedom is to you, when you want it, and with what intensity level.* ✔
3. Define and boot up the systems to run your life like a CEO.
4. Light up your scoreboard.
5. Become financially literate.
6. Learn how to scale.
7. Teach your sons and daughters to fish.
8. See how I built my real estate business.

The Three-Step Financial Freedom Process:
1. *Set a vision for your life.* ✔
2. Through awareness and sacrifice, organize your life to increase cash flow with your time.
3. Invest your money in assets that increase your cash flow.

CHAPTER 3

RUN YOUR LIFE LIKE A CEO

"If you don't have an aim, you're aimless."

—JORDAN B. PETERSON, AUTHOR

---

f you were running a business, wouldn't you be aware of as much as possible? If you weren't, how could you feel confident in making tough decisions, let alone the daily choices facing every CEO?

As a CEO, you would be very aware of your income and your expenses. You would reflect on prior months and be able to forecast upcoming months. And here's a secret. Do you want to know the most important business you'll ever run? It's your *life*.

So far, you've set a vision for your life and established your intensity level. Next, we're going to do the following:

- Forecast and stick to expenses.
- Work hard to make more.
- Be cash flow focused.
- Flip the script.
- Establish a routine.

This is the awareness step. Awareness is so important that instead of referring to a cash flow *budget*, I will be talking about cash flow *awareness*.

Without awareness, you cannot truly get organized. It is such a crucial step because at a practical level if you're not aware of the cash flow that you currently have coming in, it's really, really hard to build toward Financial Freedom and scale beyond it.

We'll start with how to forecast and review your cash flow. Remember, cash flow is calculated as follows:

Cash Flow = Income – Expenses

That's it.

Write out or input your expenses and income into a spreadsheet. Once that's done, let's continue.

Let's start with forecasting and reviewing your expenses. As you get into this chapter, keep in mind that you're not going to cut your way to Financial Freedom. If you lack discipline, it's a good place to start. Dave Ramsey has done very well advising in this realm because many people don't believe they can build that discipline. But sharpening your saving alone isn't the fastest way to Financial Freedom. Instead, you pick up speed toward your destination by increasing your cash flow by (1) increasing your income, and then later transitioning to (2) increasing your cash flow by increasing investments that increase your cash flow.

BUILD AWARENESS

If you've never done a cash flow awareness exercise, now's the time to start because you'll need a foundation to build upon. List out the expenses first. I think of there being two categories of expenses: things we need and things we want. Just as business needs to pay the mortgage, electricity, and utilities, and also has things it wants like a new marketing program (exciting but not essential), you too have needs like a student loan payment, the mortgage, and any living expenses (shelter, food, and other essentials) and wants like those extra nights out and expensive vacations. Be honest with yourself here and don't leave anything out. No use deceiving yourself as it will catch up with you later.

Monthly Cash Flow Budget

Income:

Household W2 Income	$	6,750
Other Income	$	100
Investment Income	$	350
Total Income	**$**	**7,200**

Expenses:

	Shelter	$	1,500
	Groceries	$	386
Needs	Utilities	$	150
	Transportation	$	120
	Childcare	$	1,200
	Clothing	$	350
	Vacations	$	500
Wants	Subscriptions	$	99
	Restaurants, takeout, etc.	$	400
	Personal belongings	$	250
Budgeted Expenses		$	4,955
Under/Over		$	200
Rental Expenses		$	100
Total Expenses		**$**	**5,255**

Net Monthly Cash Flow	**$**	**1,945**
Projected Month End	$	2,145
Actual Month End	**$**	**1,945**

Next, put a calendar appointment a month from today for your monthly review.

At these reviews, start by analyzing cash flow, which in the image shows $1,945. Was your cash flow higher or lower than last month? Well, obviously if it was lower than last month, let's look at the easy thing first, which is expenses.

Did you stick to your plan with expenses? Did you overspend to your plan? In the image we overspent by $200, which caused the shortfall of our cash flow projection. What was the overspend and should we include that in next month's forecast? In other words, from the vantage point of your intensity level, was that overspend something you're okay with or was that not something you were okay with? Be open with your comments. They are for you to learn from. Simple comments like "Overspent a bit!" or "Great job!" go a long way and let you criticize yourself with a sense of humor.

Sometimes there are natural unexpected events like a friend's anniversary, which you hadn't planned to attend—since you didn't know about it—but you decided to go and buy a gift for them. Don't be upset by this. You won't ever forecast everything; the important routine here is to assess how close you can get and if there are expenses you need to either allocate for the next thirty days or be more disciplined about during the next thirty days.

There may be other areas where you didn't land on forecast.

Early on, analyzing expenses may take about 50 percent of your time. But after six or nine months, you'll probably only spend about 5–10 percent on expenses.

After reviewing, forecast for the next thirty days.

Keep in mind, this is not about sharply cutting each and every expense; rather, it is about increasing your net cash flow. You can only cut so many cups of coffee. Why then do we start there? **Frankly, we start with expenses because it is the *easy* first step.** I'm sorry if you feel that planning expenses for the next thirty days is hard. This is something you've got to get in the habit of. You'll be happier knowing those expenses as a baseline.

The good news is it gets easier as you cycle yourself annually. My wife and I just did this for December 2021. We noticed that we had a note for Christmas gift shopping in December that said we should have put the spending in November to take advantage of Black Friday deals. We ended up overspending forecast in November 2020 and underspending in December 2020. This year we shifted that. Again, it's a small adjustment but understanding where your money is being allocated and spent is *very* important as you read on in this book because leftover money needs to be invested as quickly as possible. This step is helping us understand and even predict money to invest now and in the future. Remember my car breaking down? I wasn't worried about my bills and that's because of this step, which greatly helps your awareness.

After we're done allocating expenses, we get to the harder

part. After all, this step isn't called "budget." That word has a negative connotation because people associate it with living frugally and only cutting expenses. People who focus only on cutting expenses will not reach Financial Freedom as quickly as those focused on growing cash flow. Build your cash flow awareness each month and you'll start to build momentum.

WORK HARD TO MAKE MORE

Increasing income has more upside than cutting expenses. As just one example to illustrate the concept, skipping a few coffees a month will save you $20 but starting a side hustle might increase your income by $500 and make you feel less guilty about indulging in those designer drinks. In the image provided, there is $350 of investment income, which you probably aren't trading much time for. What happens if you can find a way to bump that up to $700 or $1,000 to go along with your W-2 income, which you *are* trading time for?

Early on the path to Financial Freedom, it makes a lot of sense to work hard to make more money. Yes, you're trading hours for dollars, but you need that cash flow in order to start seriously thinking about investing.

When it comes to evaluating each line item of income, in the beginning of your journey your monthly reviews may be focused on questions like:

- Did you make as much money coming in by trading your time for income?
- Did you work as hard?
- Did you put in the overtime?
- Did you develop yourself to maybe get a pay raise?
- What did you do to really increase that cash flow?

Whatever your job is, you have the opportunity to be better at it. Are you reading books and are you educating yourself to improve? I read leadership books and surrounded myself with people who were better leaders so that I could learn from them. Because I helped others my team got better results and better chances of promotion. I sought out the best at a given position in the company and was determined to decipher why they were the best and how they did it. Then I would work my ass off to beat them at those results.

If you want to get promoted quickly, if you want to earn money, it does come down to your performance and there's no better way than making yourself irreplaceable. One way to make yourself irreplaceable is to become the very best in your company at that position. When you become the very best at your position, you can almost write your own paycheck.

I would also seek to make my team the best. So if you have a team, how do you make them the best? How do you promote them? Because ultimately that'll help you.

Next thing I asked was, How do I make my boss look good? I figured the better my boss looked and the better his results, the better that would reflect on me.

Most of all, put in the work, because it'll get noticed. I was always the first one to show up and the last one to leave. My boss would never beat me to work and my boss would always leave before me. Take great pride in proving yourself through the hard work. When I was assistant to the GM, I didn't start the best, but I ended the best. When I was promoted to GM, I didn't start the best, but I became the best in my district. And when I went to District Manager, I didn't start out the best, but I got there and I did it through results.

Don't burden yourself to the point that you aren't able to naturally learn and develop a good flow. One way to remove the tension but maintain your optimism is to give yourself a bit of a time horizon. Job promotions add up over time across several years. Maybe you're in a position to express to your manager how you can be more valuable *today* for the company and you proceed immediately with asking for that raise. Maybe you need a few months to establish a pattern that you can document and show those results at the next company update. Take time to find out how to be more valuable to your company, then work your ass off to put in the time and effort, and prove your actions through results. Can you take on overtime? What about a second job? If you do take on a second job, don't let it affect the first. In my experience, if you work for a company that values performance and you exceed expectations, you'll make more this way than being average at two jobs.

Meanwhile, a side hustle with recurring revenue can add up and gain steam as well, even if it starts small. An email list of twenty-five friends and family with a bit of word of month could be two hundred and fifty by this time next year. Even selling things on the internet that are collecting dust in your basement is a very simple way to get started and boost your cash flow right now. These days, you can sell anything on the internet, it seems. Look at Gary Vaynerchuk, a CEO of a large company who still enjoys buying stuff at garage sales and reselling it online for 100 percent more than he bought it for. It's possible; it just takes hustle.

After reviewing the previous month's cash flow versus forecast, go ahead and forecast the next month.

BE CASH FLOW FOCUSED

Throughout this process, be honest. Avoid self-deception by being cash flow focused. Call yourself out when you stray from reviewing the data points. Admit to yourself when you fall short, and notice where you may need to adjust your expenses or even your intensity. Because if after a few months you are still spending about as much on wants as needs, your intensity in reality may not be a 9 or 10, it may be a 5 or 6. That's fine; maybe you are spending for the genuine aims of life. Admitting that will make it easier to reconcile overspends at the end of each month. You can always start at a 5 and move up to a 7 over time as you calibrate.

On income, if you're only trading forty hours a week, you're not a 9. A 9 intensity means you should trade more hours, get on pace to a promotion, seek overtime, maybe even take a second job or a third job, find a side hustle (educate yourself and get started), and embrace other income streams you see immediately available.

When reviewing and then forecasting, it is very helpful to have your vision and intensity statements in front of you. That way you can check reviews and forecasts and even make comments in reference to those. Occasionally, especially early on, you may adjust that intensity level, or your partner may want to. Great if you do, and even better if it is aligned with how you currently are constituted and in line with your achievable aspirations.

One thing though I can't stress enough, *do not* lie to yourself. *Do not* make excuses. I hear too often, "I'll never get to Financial Freedom; it's just not possible for me." When I ask how bad they want Financial Freedom, they say a 9 out of 10. "We will do anything, Logan." Well, then I dig in as I've shared above and find out they are spending just as much on their wants as needs. Again, that's not a 9; they are hardly a 5. If you can't sacrifice some spending now for Financial Freedom quicker later...

by definition you don't want it that bad. Then I discover they are only working forty hours a week? You've got to be kidding! You said you want this bad? Forty hours out of your one hundred sixty-eight hours in a week? Actions are not backing up the words. Sometimes I hear things are getting in the way of working longer, like taking care of kids. What are you doing while your kids are sleeping? I had two kids when doing this as well and for at least seven years did not work less than eighty hours and can't remember a full day off during that time. I found ways to do it and I found ways to still be a good dad. If you don't have time to read and educate yourself every day but you do have time for Netflix, you're not a 9 intensity. In Step One, if you say you want Financial Freedom, then put aside the excuses and get to work. Otherwise, change your intensity level and be "okay" with getting to Financial Freedom slower. Again, just don't lie to yourself—it took longer because you decided to let it take longer because you decided the sacrifices now were not worth it. The most important person to be aligned with is yourself. It makes aligning with everyone else much, much simpler.

FLIP THE SCRIPT

Either you work hard for your money or your money works hard for you. That's the difference between trading time for income and using money to create passive income.

Without passive income, it's difficult to become financially free. At some point you have to stop trading your time. Work hard to get money. Then put it into something to make it work for you. Flip the script.

Maybe at the start of your journey 80 percent of your money is earned by trading your time, and 20 percent from passive income. How can you flip the script and go 20/80?

In the image to follow you can see $1,800 is coming in by trading time while $200 is coming in passively. That's 90 percent from trading time, 10 percent from passive income. That $200 is an example of your money working hard for you. If that $200 is coming in each month, I get to use that $200 each time to make further investments.

What if you're able to find an additional investment that pays you another $200 per month? The ratio starts to shift. Now that is $1,800 by trading time and $400 from passive income. That's about 82 percent from trading time versus about 18 percent from passive sources! I will continue to emphasize this point as the book progresses: look for those investments that you understand and can control, and that pay you *now*. This brief example has just shown how quickly you can change your game by flipping the script. Either you work hard for your money or your money works hard for you.

Year 1, Age 31, Monthly Net Cash Flow

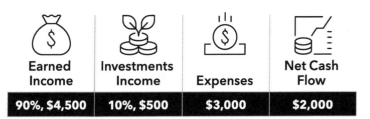

Earned Income	Investments Income	Expenses	Net Cash Flow
90%, $4,500	10%, $500	$3,000	$2,000

Year 3, Age 33, Monthly Net Cash Flow

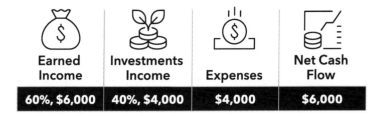

Earned Income	Investments Income	Expenses	Net Cash Flow
60%, $6,000	40%, $4,000	$4,000	$6,000

Year 5, Age 35, Monthly Net Cash Flow

Earned Income	Investments Income	Expenses	Net Cash Flow
40%, $8,000	60%, $12,000	$5,000	$15,000

Year 1, Age 31, Monthly Net Cash Flow

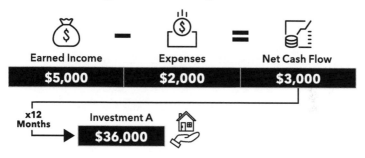

Year 3, Age 33, Monthly Net Cash Flow

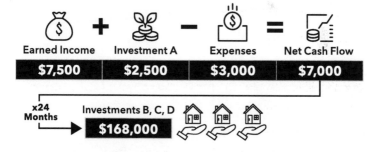

Year 5, Age 35, Monthly Net Cash Flow

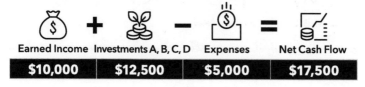

ESTABLISH A ROUTINE

The routine of reviewing your monthly results and forecasting the next month in the context of your vision and intensity starts to reinforce daily habits and decision-making. By improving the quality of your mind, you are improving your decisions, and then your life gets better. I look forward to monthly reviews with my wife because it is a chance for us to reflect, learn, and plan for the future. Be firm but fair and remember why you're doing this.

The title of this chapter is "Run Your Life like a CEO" because if you do, chances are you'll make clearer, less emotional decisions. This chapter is all about awareness. It brings to light what you need to do with your money to grow your business or in this case grow your life toward your goals. Every dollar in a business is either an expense or an investment to increase income. (I am going to say that again: every dollar...) Same applies to your personal income and life—**the most important business you will ever own is your personal life business.** As money comes in through your W-2 job and other income streams while your expenses are stable, your cash flow will increase, giving you more and more options. This is a key step, a key mindset shift, a critically important monthly awareness measurement. This step, combined with intensity of vision, will or should keep the lifestyle creep at bay. Remember, *every* month the goal is to have more cash flow than the month before. Stack that cash flow higher and higher and never look back.

By being aware of your expenses and making good decisions to keep them at the lowest level you feel comfortable at that matches your intensity and then simultaneously trading your time for more income...*that* will increase your cash flow. The goal is to beat the month before and keep growing it.

Poor people are not aware of their income and expenses and therefore tend to *spend*.

The middle class tend to understand budgets and are aware of how to use their time to make money while cutting expenses or keeping them minimal. The problem though if you stop at this step is that you are stuck only trading time for money. Even if cash flow increases, you are too focused on *saving*.

The wealthy understand how to *invest* and that is what we are going to get into in the next chapter.

YOUR PROGRESS REPORT
TOWARD FINANCIAL FREEDOM

1. *Honestly challenge norms and beliefs.* ✔
2. *Decide what Financial Freedom is to you, when you want it, and with what intensity level.* ✔
3. *Define and boot up the systems to run your life like a CEO.* ✔
4. Light up your scoreboard.
5. Become financially literate.
6. Learn how to scale.
7. Teach your sons and daughters to fish.
8. See how I built my real estate business.

The Three-Step Financial Freedom Process:
1. *Set a vision for your life.* ✔
2. *Through awareness and sacrifice, organize your life to increase cash flow with your time.* ✔
3. Invest your money in assets that increase your cash flow.

CHAPTER 4

THE SCOREBOARD

"Money is just a way to keep score."

—ERIC S. RAYMOND,
OPEN-SOURCE SOFTWARE DEVELOPER

---

recently started coaching a couple in their late forties who
knew since their thirties that their vision was to reach Financial
Freedom by age fifty-two. They picked that year because their
kids would be out of high school and out of the house, and then
they could travel. They also had a cash flow budget.

They had a vision, Step One, and a cash flow budget, Step Two.

On to Step Three. I was excited because this is the third step, which I call the Scoreboard, where all that prior work starts to come together. The Scoreboard does three things: (1) it lists your assets and liabilities, (2) it provides a total net worth, and most importantly, (3) it shows you the *productivity* of each asset and liability. **It's the step where you get to make your money work harder for you.**

I relate to the concept of a scoreboard from my college basketball days.

For the couple, there was a bump in the road.

I wish I'd met them sooner in life so that we could have avoided what happened next. They had had their system in place for about seventeen years already by the time we got to talking.

I'll cut to the chase: their Scoreboard was dark. They didn't know if they were winning or losing. And there were only five quarters, five years left on their original vision. Would they be able to exit the rat race?

Remember what I said in the previous section: what matters most about your assets is whether they align with your vision.

Now, even though they had a financial advisor, almost all of their investments were tied up in their 401(k), almost 90 percent. Seven figures in that vehicle.

That's a huge problem because you can't access the 401(k) until fifty-nine and a half years of age, at least not without a significant penalty, and they had planned to once they reached age fifty-two. That's a seven-year difference. We did the math on taking some of the money earlier but it actually meant their Financial Freedom wouldn't come until about age fifty-five.

They slouched a little and you could see the realization in their eyes. All that time and effort across all those years. They made the sacrifices, they worked long hours, they set the vision, and they made good decisions with expenses. Unfortunately, they didn't make good decisions with their investments. Even if they took out the 401(k), the penalties would set them back three years, until fifty-five. That seriously threw off their long-held plans for Financial Freedom.

That decision violated the principle of alignment.

That lack of alignment was a hard pill to swallow. But they had to confront it. They faced the reality and they are moving forward. What other choice do they have? It's admirable when people realize the error of their ways and correct it, even if that takes effort and time.

If you're reading this and you haven't yet made this mistake, please do take heed. You must be prepared to continuously question your own financial understanding—remain humble!—and don't let yourself be persuaded by financial advisors or random blog posts or TV experts who are not providing data that is put through logical consideration toward a conclusion. This way you can ensure you stay true to working hard for your money but also be ready to turn the corner and make your money work hard for you too.

To balance that negative story with a positive example, consider my mom and dad. At age fifty-eight, they were still seven years from retirement on the normal track society suggests. But after working with me, they opted to invest in their first real estate property and things changed for them.

You see, they were planning to sell their current home, which was fully paid off, and buy a new home with 100 percent equity, no mortgage required. After a lot of discussions I helped them see how buying a real estate property would not only help them pay their new mortgage—they put 20 percent down and took on 80 percent as a mortgage—but also begin to provide passive income. They were against the idea initially because it went counter to their idea of being financially free. They didn't want any debts! After all, they'd spent the last thirty years working hard to pay off their first house. It was daunting to take out another thirty-year mortgage. Based on how you've been programmed, does taking out this amount of debt also feel uncomfortable?

They could have bought their new home outright. But by only putting down 20 percent they had extra money to invest in real estate.

Only two years later, they had sixteen units and that let them retire a full five years ahead of the original retirement plan. In fact, the income from those investments produced as much passive income as all the other investments they had invested in during their W-2 working years.

While taking out another thirty-year mortgage was daunting, it was only daunting because my parents, as maybe you were as well, were programmed to think about only debt and expenses. I give my parents a lot of credit. They opened their minds to consider thinking differently about the possibilities of real estate investment with new information. There are two sides to debt if considering investments. There's the income side as well. Once they understood the income was much larger than the expense, that there was an overall net positive cash flow, they dedicated a lot of time to further understanding real estate investments.

They had a vision and were organized, but they weren't yet doing Step Three, which is finding the right investments. I'm so proud of them for opening their minds, then working their butts off mentally, so late in life, to understand this investment.

NET WORTH = ASSETS - LIABILITIES

The process of building your Scoreboard begins by listing your assets and liabilities. As with your cash flow budget, on a spreadsheet is probably best.

Net Worth			
ASSETS		**LIABILITIES**	
Personal Home	$ 200,000	Home Mortgage	$ 150,000
Vehicle	$ 20,000	Vehicle Loan	$ 10,000
401(k)	$ 50,000	Investment Property Mortgage	$ 110,000
Investment Property A	$ 150,000	School Loans	$ 40,000
Savings	$ 15,000	Credit Cards	$ 5,300
ASSETS TOTAL	**$ 435,000**	**LIABILITIES TOTAL**	**$ 315,300**
NET WORTH	**$ 119,700**		

To ensure you don't leave any out, keep the following definitions in mind.

WHAT IS AN ASSET?

Any resource with financial value that is controlled by a company, country, or individual. There is a broad range of assets that you or your business may own, create, or benefit from, including real estate, cash, office equipment, goodwill, investments, patents, inventory, and more.

WHAT ARE LIABILITIES?

Legally binding obligations that are payable to another person or entity. Recorded on the right side of the balance sheet, liabilities include loans, accounts payable, mortgages, deferred revenues, bonds, warranties, and accrued expenses.

WHAT IS NET WORTH?

Net worth is a measure of wealth. Net worth is the sum of all assets owned by a person or a company, minus any obligations or liabilities.

Net Worth = Assets − Liabilities

You have most of what you need to get started, but let me share a brief story from my journey so you understand that the opportunity to benefit from using a Scoreboard is available to anyone, no matter the starting point.

THE PROCESS AND ROUTINE

When it comes to developing a process and routine for your Scoreboard, consider these three dimensions for each investment:

1. How well do I understand and control that investment?
2. Did that investment increase in net worth?
3. How much cash flow did that investment produce last month?

After a few months on the first question, you'll have a good idea of your understanding and level of control and won't spend much time here.

On the second question, surprises aren't good. If something differed from what you forecasted, slow down to figure out why.

The third question might be the most important. What matters most is how much income those investments produced. Because if you want Financial Freedom, you will need investments to give you money so that you can stop merely trading your time for income.

Be aware that some investments appear as both assets and liabilities. A real estate property will be an asset in terms of its equity and a liability in terms of its mortgage. So, did the overall investment produce cash flow? If the net impact is positive, that is obviously the passive income from that investment.

Each month, after evaluating your cash flow, review your net worth and productivity of your net worth.

The objective is to increase your net worth month over month. Equally important is your intention to use that increasing net worth to improve your cash flow. You do that by putting money into investments that pay you now.

NEGATIVE $40,000

Before I learned about the productivity of money, which I'll define very shortly, I didn't even know what an asset or a liability was. I was renting an apartment.

It was a shock to find myself *negative* $40,000 when my score-board turned on. Maybe a lot of you are feeling that right now. But once I got into the process and started to check in on that scoreboard each month, it was just a little bit closer to zero. My wife and I were on the move.

Once the Scoreboard was on, we were no longer in the dark. I understood that we could stay down or get in the game. Those were really the only two choices.

And once I chose to get in the game, I had to ask myself, Why was I really down $40,000? The answer came to me: because I was only playing defense. I was saving, I was trying to reduce my debt, and putting money in a 401(k). **I was working hard for my money but my money wasn't working hard for me.** My money wasn't *productive*. It wasn't increasing my cash flow and paying me now. I wasn't on offense yet. I was treading water in the face of inflation, taxes, and unwanted fees.

The magnitude of the negative $40,000 was mainly due to student debt, because I took the path that society offered—go to college.

But you can only dwell so long on the what-ifs, the regrets, the mistakes. My first look shocked me, but from another van-tage point, that awareness was *good* because it gave me motiva-tion to start changing things, *every single day*. Each day is a game that I try to win. I tried to move my net worth closer to zero dollars. Even if it was just a couple dollars closer to zero, that was a win! In eighteen months, we were at zero—from negative $40,000 to $0—and that was a big win.

I also took one day each month to review what wasn't working and what was, and kept going. That turned into the process and routine we've already discussed.

Early on, equipped with our vision and cash flow awareness, it was easy to cut expenses to increase cash flow and therefore start inching up on the scoreboard.

Soon, however, it became glaringly obvious that we could only cut so much and kept crawling up at a pace too slow for comfort. We had goals to meet! So I started paying more attention to income: we worked overtime, we worked longer, we gave plasma, we earned promotions, and we watched happily as the scoreboard continued to move up faster. **We were spending all of our time to improve our score until we found we had no time left over.** I wondered, *Was there a way to accelerate this process?* From Calculus in high school I knew that the *rate of change* mattered. We were moving at a good pace, but I wanted it to get faster each month. If we didn't have any time left to trade for dollars, how could we do that?

Then it dawned on me: we could use our assets to earn money, too.

We carefully turned to the assets we already had and started to assess them, including my 401(k), my Roth, my savings, and even the liabilities we had or didn't have. At the time I didn't

Investments, Year 1, 31 Years of Age

Investments, Year 3, 33 Years of Age

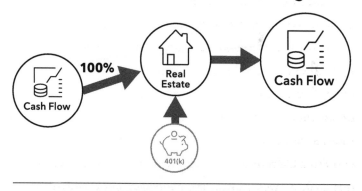

Investments, Year 5, 35 Years of Age (RE Has Increased Productivity)

have a good financial education, so I turned to books to better understand those investments and my options generally.

But it was only when I understood and applied the principle of *productivity*—how hard each dollar is working—that things started to accelerate, and ultimately why we reached Financial Freedom much sooner than planned.

Cash-on-Cash Returns Measure Productivity

It's a lot of work to establish a clear vision for Financial Freedom, what you want by when through which sacrifices. If you've done that, good work! And it takes will and effort to put the process in motion of running your life like a CEO. If you've done that, *great*. Don't squander that effort by *only* focusing on trading your time for dollars, or *only* watching the net cash flow.

We're getting to a part of this I really, really enjoy, because it is powerful. This is the part where you assess your assets and liabilities and make them work hard for you to increase your monthly cash flow. You can't do that unless those assets and liabilities are paying you *now*. If they are doing *both* of those things, they probably are quite *productive*.

Productivity is measured by **Cash-on-Cash** (ConC) returns. ConC return is more meaningful than return on investment (ROI) because **you have that money in your hands ready to reinvest right now.** That's how you really light up your scoreboard.

Let's take a moment to unpack the difference between ConC return and ROI.

ConC return **tracks the amount of cash flow compared with the amount of cash invested in an investment.** Simply said, take the amount of net cash flow you receive for the year and divide that by the cost to buy or put additional capital in the asset. This is basically how fast the money you invested will come back to you. This is key because it's possible to get back that money you invested while still controlling the asset.

For me, productivity relates directly to the concept of production. Is this asset *producing* something now? The metric to track here is ConC return. *Not* return on investment. ConC, not ROI. With ConC you are answering the question, *When you invest cash in an investment, what percentage of that cash do you get back for a given time period?*

Investor Kevin O'Leary put it this way: "Money is my military, each dollar a soldier. I never send my money into battle unprepared and undefended. I send it to conquer and take currency prisoner and bring it back to me."

Make every dollar count by tracking its productivity by measuring ConC returns monthly and annually. Ask those soldiers how many prisoners they've taken *today*, not twenty years from now. I hear people say things like, "My return on investment in my 401(k) was fantastic this year at 20 percent!" Well, that's great but let me ask you this: How much did you invest in your 401(k) and how much did it pay you back on that investment this year? They usually give me a look of confusion. "Well, I didn't get anything back, I just know it grew by 20 percent." That's great, but where is it? Can you control that 20 percent increase? Further, can you use it to reinvest into something else? When will you receive that 20 percent increase and is that okay with you?

To sum up: Net worth is how you keep score, but we will *not* focus on the net worth itself, nor only how it is changing, but how the *productivity* of the line items, both assets and liabilities, are changing from month to month, using ConC return as the key metric. Your net worth is only as good as the speed at which it's paying you now if you want to retire as fast as possible.

MORE ATTENTION TO YOUR BEST INVESTMENTS

Each month, go line by line. How productive was the first investment? The next? And the next? What made them productive if they were? What made them less productive if they weren't? This exercise is to discover how to make your assets and liabilities feed your cash flow.

What action steps can you take after reviewing?

1. You can educate yourself further on that asset.
2. Get rid of that asset.
3. Off-load that asset and put proceeds into a different asset that produces income.

To drill in on each asset and liability, answer the questions:

- **Do I understand it?** Do you understand the tax implications of each asset and liability, do you understand where your money is invested, the possible fees, the risk? Can you predict its returns?

- **Do I control it?** Do you have control over this asset as to what you do with the money? For example, if you wanted to, could you sell the investment, could you move the money, could you reallocate it? If so, is there a penalty or does this cost money? If your money is in a stock or company, can you control the decisions that company makes?

And finally...

- **How can I make it more productive?** Is this asset paying you now? Can you make this asset work harder for you, today?

Starting out, some things I just didn't know. For example, I didn't understand the 401(k). If you don't understand it, you shouldn't put your money in it. That's my rule. Make it your rule too. You'll thank me one day. Don't get me wrong, I started to understand how a 401(k) worked but I still couldn't pinpoint exactly where and into what companies my money was being invested. Furthermore, your 401(k)'s asset size may increase, but it will not be productive for you because it cannot pay you now—that means zero cash flow today.

If a financial advisor helps you understand it, great, but if you are more confused after that meeting with the financial advisor, consider that and take responsibility for that understanding yourself. Ultimately it is you, not the advisor, who has to live with the decision.

I didn't understand stocks either. After starting to educate myself, I realized I couldn't figure out how a company's decision-making affected the stock price. Even if I did understand the decisions of the company, I still didn't have any influence over those decisions. I tried reading annual reports to better understand the companies, but in the end I just didn't feel I had enough information or control. To me, stocks were like gambling! I could read all I wanted about the company but if the CEO tweeted something people didn't like, I could lose significant value. How crazy is that?

After you understand each asset and liability, ask, Can I predict it? Understanding usually allows you to predict. I love when I hear financial advisors talk about understanding a 401(k) and the predictions on returns. Or a friend who talks about stocks and how he understands the company so well and can predict the returns. When I say understand, I *really* mean understand it. Let me be frank: I understand a lot about 401(k)s—I understand how they work, I understand the fees, and I even understand the different options they allow you to put your money in. I understand the difference between a Roth 401(k) and a traditional 401(k). However, this is not the understanding I am talking about. I am talking about understanding the investments your money is aligned with and how those investments will produce a predictable return.

Make note of how productive each asset and liability is at the moment. If you have a credit card debt of $1,000 that is charging 22 percent interest, that is a strong negative in the productivity column—to be exact, its productivity is negative 22 percent. If you have savings available, which are likely producing very low productivity, you could pay off that $1,000 to improve the productivity of that batch of funds. The only reason I can think of not to pay off that $1,000 at 22 percent interest is if you have a low-risk option that has a bigger positive return. In my case, after learning a lot about real estate and scaling the business, I know that I can reliably get a property to, on average, a 37 percent ConC return after two to three years.

RULES OF THUMB FOR DEBT

Stay grounded with rules of thumb.

With experience I recommend you develop your own rules of thumb that work for you and have a trend in favor of making you happier and increasing the productivity of each piece of your net worth.

Take debt, for example.

I simply think of debt as an expense that costs me X amount each month. So, just like I taught you in the previous chapter, that is important to understand because it will hurt cash flow... but cash flow has two levers, not one. The other lever is income. So I like to think of debt in terms of how much income this debt can produce for me if that changes productivity from negative to positive—that's step one in considering debt. Then I need to assess the relationship with risk and how likely that income will continue to beat the debt expense.

This way of thinking led me to take out a loan on my Tesla that I originally owned outright because that loan was only about 2 percent while I could turn around and invest that $100,000 for a healthier return, thus making that $100,000 more productive. This is a mindset shift. You have to remember, it's about cash flow and if you're using debt to buy investments, you should also have income. If income is greater than the expense, then you are now making that money more productive. If taking out debt on a fully paid-off vehicle scares you, stay open minded and read on.

Don't fear debt; seek to understand its use in each and every case.

When it comes to returns, I want to challenge myself to at least make investments that reliably return 12 percent or more (because that keeps me well above historical average inflation as a starting point). As stated, after twenty-four months my real estate properties tend to return 30 percent or more. For me, as I learned and operated the business, my returns increased. That's common sense. As you become experienced and even an expert, you will have a variety of skills in your toolbox and be able to notice patterns and opportunities others may have missed. Some of those will come as a result of the process you follow and the systems you put in place around you, while others are more intangible and a kind of gift based on your curiosity and interest. Keep learning and keep exploring. Stay a student forever.

WHAT HAPPENS IF YOU HAVE SLOW-MOVING INVESTMENTS?

So far we've discussed ideal investments, but you probably aren't already *holding* that position, or you might not have picked up this book. Not to worry. I was in some slow-moving investment vehicles myself when I was starting out.

On the early part of the road from negative $40,000 to Financial Freedom, I had a 401(k), a Roth, and too much in a savings account. I didn't understand or control the 401(k) and the Roth and neither paid me now. They were not improving the speed of cash flow and my net worth trend each month.

What to do?

First, like a basketball coach assessing his players, *bench* the bad investments—that means you stop continuing to invest in them. Second, *cut* the bad investments: change the investments to better investments. Third, invest in your best *star* investments.

BENCH THE BAD INVESTMENTS

Bad investments are those you neither understand nor control and which do not pay you now.

Stop putting money into those investments. I didn't say *cut* them, yet. Meanwhile, continue to save and stack money while you educate yourself further on better options for that money.

In my case, I stopped continuing to contribute to my 401(k). I still had the 401(k), but I wasn't pouring additional money into it. This was also the time to pick up a book and educate myself. It hurt to discover that I'd been allocating funds to an investment that didn't align with my vision for Financial Freedom. But no more excuses, it was time to learn. For me, I really started to like what I was seeing in real estate investing. At the beginning, there wasn't a book or blog post I didn't like on the topic. Even perspectives I later decided were unhelpful gave me something to ponder at the outset.

CUT THE BAD INVESTMENTS

After you're confident in how much the benched investments are producing for you, it's time to consider cutting them.

Warren Buffett describes asset diversification as a defensive strategy for those who don't really know what they are doing. The Oracle of Omaha summed it up nicely when he said, "Diversification may preserve wealth, but concentration builds wealth."

But I go one step further: don't be afraid to be bold and outright *cut* bad investments. For me, I spoke with my CPA and began the process of taking the cash out of my 401(k). I incurred penalties, but I had ideas for how I would use the money, and I would likely not be writing this book if those ideas didn't turn out fairly well. However, as I review my own timeline, it is true that I didn't do this immediately. I was a little hesitant because I hadn't yet proven to myself that I could generate solid returns elsewhere.

INVEST IN YOUR STAR INVESTMENTS

A big reason to cut your bad investments is so you have more room to invest in your top performing investments, your stars. Once you find the trifecta—investment vehicles you understand, can control, and which pay you now—start going all in.

With each additional investment within an asset class you go into, continue to up your execution. That's the way to yield the most productivity from your investment. Investing the traditional way through diversification is about preservation of wealth; however, we are working to not only build wealth but build cash flow passively. This is done through the questions I already shared: understanding, control, and money now to allow for velocity.

WHAT HAPPENS WHEN YOU REACH FINANCIAL FREEDOM?

If you can increase cash flow and buy assets that pay you today, that is the quickest route to Financial Freedom. When your money is working harder for you than you are working for it, you will accelerate your trajectory.

When you hit Financial Freedom, you can do one of two things. Slowly stop trading your time for money. Or slowly spend a bit more on expenses, perhaps bringing in a few more of your wants.

Consider your monthly cash flow is $10,000 this month. In a few months, through increased productivity of your assets, your income goes up to $11,000. You can either scale back to $10,000 by spending $1,000 more on things you want in the month *or* you could make $1,000 less (by working less).

Be thankful that you get to make that decision and realize there are two levers to pick from. By the way, there is a third lever too that you should have been pulling every time on the way to Financial Freedom. That is, you keep working hard, you keep expenses low, and you now cash-flow the $11,000 and are able to spin the wheel faster. Stack money faster so you can then invest faster and that will allow the monthly cash flow to push past 11k faster. This cycle we will talk about later but the third lever is fun too when you pay attention to cash flow. It makes the sacrifices more worth it.

At this juncture, my wife and I decided to take back some of our time instead of spending more on expenses. We had learned how to live within our needs and were enjoying it. But it's up to you! For us, our first step here was retiring my wife from her W-2 job. A second kid was on the way, which meant time back for her to reallocate toward the family but also put more energy towards our passive streams of income.

One day you could get to a place where your assets are creating that net cash flow that you are good with to the point that you can quit all your jobs where you are trading the time.

Keep cash flow as the target. Stabilize your expenses and increase your income. Each month, raise cash flow higher than the previous month. Do that until you reach Financial Freedom. *Then* you really have options.

PLAY THE GAME OF LIFE YOUR WAY

Don't forget that you've already decided to play the game of life, *your way*. So when you set up this scoreboard, light it up so that it lights up and guides you on *your* path, not someone else's.

When cash flow is there, we have *options*. We are putting hard-earned cash into investments that produce further options. Compare that against putting all your eggs into a 401(k) that tells *you* when you can retire. Shouldn't *you* be deciding?

The Scoreboard can keep track of much more than your net worth—consider all the other domains of life!—but that is a fine place to start. Most people don't understand a net worth statement, never update it, or only update it when the bank asks (maybe once a year). Meanwhile, the wealthiest people update their net worth once a month. It will become part of your process and part of the process you enjoy.

I want to emphasize this. The goal is to grow the net worth over the month before and at the same time grow net worth with the intention to use that net worth to grow cash flow. *Now.* The more net worth you have, the easier you can find creative ways to increase cash flow. Especially if it is in the right investments. You can't increase cash flow unless those investments are paying you now. Don't lose sight of that.

YOUR PROGRESS REPORT
TOWARD FINANCIAL FREEDOM

1. *Honestly challenge norms and beliefs.* ✔
2. *Decide what Financial Freedom is to you, when you want it, and with what intensity level.* ✔
3. *Define and boot up the systems to run your life like a CEO.* ✔
4. *Light up your scoreboard.* ✔
5. Become financially literate.
6. Learn how to scale.
7. Teach your sons and daughters to fish.
8. See how I built my real estate business.

The Three-Step Financial Freedom Process:

1. *Set a vision for your life.* ✔
2. *Through awareness and sacrifice, organize your life to increase cash flow with your time.* ✔
3. *Invest your money in assets that increase your cash flow.* ✔

CHAPTER 5

YOUR MONEY SHOULD MOVE

"Give a man a fish and you feed him today. Teach every boy how to fish and you will rarely find any man short of fish."
—ANONYMOUS

A few years into working for the Fortune 50 company, I was talking to my manager about money, and he could tell I was frustrated. "Logan, you need to read a book!" he told me. Why was he telling me that and why did it help so much?

I hadn't considered reading a book about money, not seriously, until then. At the time, I was working very hard, paying off debt, and trying to move up in the company, but I was looking at my scoreboard from the overall perspective, not from the perspective of productivity on an asset-by-asset and liability-by-liability basis. To this day I am very grateful for that simple encouragement. Because I wanted to score faster. And if my wife and I were to ever reach our goal of Financial Freedom by forty-five, we needed to score faster. The way to do that best, that I've found so far, is to *velocitize* your money through cashflow-driving assets.

Right there and then, I set out to be literate and to always be learning.

Growing up in a working-class neighborhood in small-town Wisconsin, there wasn't a lot of financial literacy in the water. That was okay. People worked hard. They helped each other. They loved their family and their neighbor. Great lessons, but very few about money.

Knowing what I know now, it is a shame they weren't taught or shown the rules of this game. Maybe they had an inkling, but they opted out. It's your choice how to spend the time that is given to you. You don't get to choose what challenges come your way, only your attitude toward those events. You get to choose how to perceive them. Maybe these are important trials to overcome. In overcoming those tests, you add skills to your skill box and become a better version of yourself equipped to scale yet steeper mountains.

Why don't most people want to question their financial literacy? Why don't most people educate themselves? It comes down to fear and convenience. Some people fear what they don't know. They fear they will uncover many mistakes they've made. They don't want to have to look at themselves in the mirror. Others aren't afraid, but they are attached to convenience. And it would be *inconvenient* to have to admit they don't know that they aren't financially literate and that this is decreasing their happiness. They justify that they are just fine where they are. They argue (1) It will take years to become literate, or (2) I'm just fine the way I am, and even though I'm living paycheck to paycheck, there's not really that much that can be done about it, or (3) I want to learn about investments but there's a football game on Sunday to watch. Richard Hawkins said, "Enslavement by illusion is comfortable; it is the liberation by truth that people fear."

This is key: just because you weren't literate until now, doesn't mean you can't change it. It took me until my midtwenties to realize I was ill-equipped to evaluate the new information coming at me. These days, so much information is at our fingertips. You will do well to find a method or routine that works for you of inputs, processing, and outputs.

I read a book a month starting the same year my wife and I decided we would become financially free by forty-five.

How to decide which book? It almost doesn't matter. It matters more that you *start*. Ask people you respect (or people who are where you want to be) for recommendations. Read the introductions of books for free online. Search for free PDFs or type a book's name into archive.org. I personally like to have a book in hand, whether from the library or bought from a bookstore. Then I can mark it up and keep notes on the things that vex me or intrigue me in a way I can't yet verbalize. I return to those notes and highlights to ponder them more deeply. Sometimes that simple routine leads to breakthroughs in my real estate business.

Keep reading until you love to learn. You don't need to read a whole book in one sitting (though, be my guest if you can). Short of that, why not read for nine minutes every morning and another nine minutes before bed? That's eighteen minutes a day, and will get you through an average book on money, investments, finance, or anything else in about a month. Some people say, "But Logan, a whole month to read just one book?" Yes, but let me ask you: how many books did you read last year? In my first year of this approach, I read twelve, one per month. After that, I became more ambitious and more curious, and read more widely. And then you start to notice patterns between books; you begin to dissect the differences between various authors and their recommended approaches. Like Bruce Lee picked up new fighting techniques from his opponents, you adopt what you like and leave the rest. But you have to start somewhere. And you get out of things what you put into them. Some call that an investment.

In this chapter, I'll share the biggest lessons I learned from all those books, which are a mirror—you could even say "the answers to the test" from Chapter 1. These lessons were key because they broke my mindset on the money tips I grew up believing and maybe the tips you still believe today.

1. Penny invested, penny earned.
2. Debt should not be feared, it should be understood.
3. Pick an investment you understand.
4. Think for yourself and solve problems.
5. Know what you don't know.

Before proceeding, let's review the levels of financial *literacy* so that you can self-assess as you go forward into the next few months.

Level one:

- You don't understand how much you are making or spending.
- You have little awareness of your assets or liabilities, possibly even ignorance about your credit card debt.
- Typically, you're living paycheck to paycheck and spending more than you make.

- You are generally in the "Spend" category.
- If you're at this level, someone like Dave Ramsey may help—perhaps start with *The Total Money Makeover*.

Level two:

- You have a general idea of your cash flow and how it is trending.
- You tend to focus the majority of time on cutting expenses and saving money, rather than on alternative ways to expand your income; saving money makes you feel like you are getting ahead. You want to pay off your house and hate all debt.
- You work hard for your money but have no real clue how to make your money work hard for you, other than a vague idea of what others have told you, like throwing money into a 401(k).
- You are generally in the "Save" category.
- If this is you, this is when you should open your mind to concepts in this book.

Level three:

- You understand the cash flow budget from an awareness and predictable vantage point, not as a saving function;

predictability allows you to understand the rate of
money you'll then be able to invest.

- You spend time adding multiple streams of income and
  understand the difference between passive and active.
- Your earned income assets are working harder and harder.
- You understand and apply the concept of the productivity
  of money or velocity of money versus compound interest.
- You are generally in the "Invest" category.
- You pay more attention to how your assets are growing
  now than your monthly cash flow budget. You ensure all
  of your money is moving, never staying still.

Even though most don't move into level three, you *can*, and
you will. These financial *literacy* skills tend to correlate to your
progress through the three-step approach to Financial Freedom,
although your mileage may vary.

I repeat, the above is how I think about financial *literacy* and
this is distinct from the three-step Financial Freedom process,
which is about setting a vision, getting organized, and making
your money work hard for you. Where they intersect is on the
last point, the productivity of money.

When you read a book, you have the opportunity to question or reflect on what you're reading. If you merely take the
author's word for it, you are actually, in part, giving away your
chance to learn.

As you read new information, ask yourself:

- *Does what I'm reading make sense?*
- *Does it in any way violate common sense?*
- *Does it contend with my intuition?*
- *What assumptions is the author making in their arguments?*
- *Are there any flaws in logic?*
- *Do their conclusions follow from the arguments?*
- *Are there alternative solutions to those being proposed?*
- *What isn't being talked about that might be?*

Oftentimes, what you read is a seed to the action you will soon after take. A seed is critical. An apple tree bearing fruit begins with a tiny seed planted just right, in friendly soil and the right climate.

If you are not a big reader, don't be too hard on yourself as you begin to read. You may have issues concentrating. You might want to step away and do something else. But, remember, you're planting seeds. If you are not paying attention, you will plant the wrong seeds in the wrong soil in the wrong climate.

There's no reason to tell others what you are reading while you are doing so. The work is your work, for your eyes only. This is a guardrail so that you are not reading for someone else, but for *yourself*. If you tell others, you may fall into the trap of being the person who is often heard talking about reading books—for which you may be praised—but seldom reading them.

You may well be facing several fears at this stage in the process toward Financial Freedom. Maybe you are recognizing all the mistakes you've made in the past. All the times you've squandered money, and the fights you've had with your spouse because you didn't want to admit you'd done so.

But the road to Financial Freedom passes through a town called Financial Literacy. You don't need a financial advisor to become literate. Take a load off. Look around. Grab a chair and stay awhile.

As you review these sections, remember that this book is not about keeping your money stagnant; this book is about velocitizing your money. Your money should *move*.

SOCIETY TEACHES YOU TO PLAY DEFENSE

Society has imprinted on your brain the instinct to be defensive. Protect what you have instead of going for more. Listen to the experts instead of the crazy ones. Stick to sure bets instead of the bold, volatile plays.

Save money. Avoid debt like the plague. Put your money in a 401(k).

Defense is fine. And we all instinctively know how to do it. Defense is deep within us. Defense is survival.

But what about the other side of the game? That's what the Scoreboard is about.

The Scoreboard in the previous chapter is about how to play offense.

Figure out which of your assets are producing, which investments are working. Do you understand them? Are they efficient? Are they effective? Do they align with your overall strategy?

Society teaches defense. It's okay to play some defense, but offense is where you want to spend the majority of your time. Figure out which of your assets are producing, which investments are working. Do you understand them? Are they efficient? Are they effective? Do they align with your overall strategy?

Sometimes we feel that it is safer to play defense than to take risks and drive for more offense. Unfortunately, playing it safe can also come with significant risks that I'll touch on in the next chapter. For now, this illustration can help: Many people think the safest place for their money is just saving it in the bank. You can't lose it in an investment that way...but is that really safe? Consider inflation rates in 2021. Consider opportunity costs. What other questions come to mind? Does a million dollars go the same distance it used to? A retiree in 1992 with a million dollars in the bank would probably have been pretty happy. Are people retiring with a million dollars feeling the same level of comfort in 2022? Only looking at inflation, the value of the 1992 dollar was worth more than twice as much as it is today.

Saving is not safe: it is risky and it is a great way for you to lose your money slowly without even knowing it until it is too late.

PRECEPT #1, REIMAGINED
PENNY INVESTED, PENNY EARNED

Robert Kiyosaki said, "Saving is losing." And he's right.

Let's start by looking at banks. Then inflation.

To start with, banks usually charge an annual fee to keep your account open or to have a credit card through them. Banks can then make money with the money you put in by loaning it out. While you make a fraction of a percent in interest in generous cases, the bank could be making 1 to 5 percent by loaning that amount. There is a reason banks and insurance companies have the biggest buildings in every city. It's called arbitrage and they are using your money to do it. They are *moving* money and taking advantage of the velocity of money. They do it over and over again making their actual returns *very* high while keeping the money you gave them to do this and giving you terrible returns.

"Come save your money with us!" they say. Come in and keep your money still and stagnant. It's free to open a checking account. (Is it really free?)

Have you ever questioned what is being done with that money as it "sits" in the bank? How do banks make their money? Are banks putting their money in the bank? Why not?

I personally didn't understand what banks do with money. I didn't realize there was something called fractional banking. I didn't understand what commercial banks do once I deposit my money with them. The fact is that if everyone went to withdraw from the bank today, they might only have about 10 percent of everyone's money, possibly less.

If this is true, it begs the questions: Where is the money going? What are they doing with it? What would happen if everyone wanted to withdraw their money at once? Why don't banks put their money in banks?

Banks are a business and they are taking your money, loaning it out, and making money off your money on the spread. They actually keep very little of your money in their bank. They don't want your money sitting; they want it moving and being loaned out so while you are sleeping and happy about your money being "safe," they are thinking about how to take your money and loan it out as many times as possible before you ask for it back and at a much higher interest rate than what you are receiving.

And safe is a strong word, considering the FDIC is only insuring your money up to about $250,000. You may be thinking, well that's fine, I don't need more than that anyways. I thought that too.

Now, am I trying to say banks are bad, or that banks are evil? Not at all. In fact, you should learn from banks. I'm trying to help teach you what few people do and since most don't ask what actually is being done with your money when you give it to the bank, this is an important lesson. Never give your hard-earned money to anyone, any investment, or any account without understanding it.

Banks are fantastic when you understand how they work! In fact, banks are my biggest partner in my main business, real estate. No need to reinvent the wheel here. Once I understood what banks are doing with money, I started doing the same thing! Again, there is a reason they have the biggest and best buildings in every major city. They are giving you something like .001 percent interest on your money you "lent" them...then using it to give to someone like me and charging 3 percent. So now they are making 2.999 percent on money that's not even theirs. Brilliant, actually! And when I pay the 2.999 percent each month, they loan it out again! What about me, you say? Well, I'm taking your money they lent me at 3 percent, and moving it again by putting it into real estate investments that have averaged over 30 percent in ConC returns that pay me now. So I can pay back the bank and still have money left over with the spread for myself. Now money that wasn't mine, passing through an investment, pays back the money that's not mine and turns the money left to mine.

How's my spread looking? Now you know why I love banks, why I learned arbitration from them, and how I make huge spreads on your money in the bank.

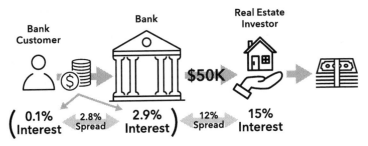

Bank Customer

Bank

Real Estate Investor

$50K

$\left(\begin{array}{cc} \textbf{0.1\%} & \text{2.8\%} \\ \textbf{Interest} & \text{Spread} \end{array} \right.$ $\begin{array}{c} \textbf{2.9\%} \\ \textbf{Interest} \end{array} \left.\begin{array}{cc} \text{12\%} \\ \text{Spread} \end{array} \right)$ $\begin{array}{c} \textbf{15\%} \\ \textbf{Interest} \end{array}$

From one perspective, the bank customer risks the least. From another, isn't he risking the most once inflation and retirement are fully considered?

Here's the takeaway: whenever you put money in a bank, remember what they are doing with it. Instead, imagine ways to move that money quickly. Dream up ways to invest it. Then you can be in a position to ask them for money!

What's more, there's the matter of inflation.

To this day I do not understand why the concept of inflation is not taught in public schools more. If a personal finance class cannot fit into the schedule, why not add a one-hour segment in a single day of history class? Inflation has been a serious factor since Nixon took the US Dollar off the gold standard in 1971. Today, inflation is calculated using the Consumer Price Index (CPI), first introduced in 1913, but inflation can be estimated prior to that through other means.

Since the US Dollar came off the gold standard, inflation continues to be a perennial problem. (With a fixed asset like gold or other precious metals, with which to tie a currency's value, inflation is less of an issue.) At present, if your theory of money, wealth, and value doesn't account for inflation, you're leaving out a major variable in your calculations. Moving off the gold standard is rarely discussed or understood but you should research this, understand this, and question how this affects your current investment strategy.

Inflation is not difficult to understand and it's a tragedy it isn't taught to kids, who will easily understand it with basic examples. Teaching it to kids also yields the benefit of more adults knowing *before* making big decisions about their money. If your sons and daughters are not learning this in school, you have the ability and responsibility to teach them.

The year 2021 has provided a significant real-life demonstration of the power of inflation. Generally speaking, if the money supply increases, then the value of each unit of currency decreases. When the Fed prints money, and between 2020 and 2021 they printed trillions, with a "t", there is a large increase in the money supply. In fact, as of May 2020, over 40 percent of the total US Dollars in circulation were printed in the prior twelve months. This is why 2021 has seen quarter-century highs in the inflation rate, well above 5 percent. It's remarkable it has remained this low as the true inflation rate is actually higher, perhaps around 20 percent but they don't report everything they should when assessing the reported rate. Without complete and accurate info, how can you start to logically process it to develop a viewpoint for yourself? What does that mean for the money in your savings account?

For a simple example, let's put inflation at 5 percent. If you had $10,000 in your savings account to start the year, that same number of dollars is actually worth $9,500 by year end. "But wait!" you say, as you check your account and still see the $10,000 on your digital balance, "I still have ten thousand dollars." Correct, but what has happened to the prices of nearly every product and service in the marketplace, from gasoline to groceries to your energy bill? The purchasing power of that $10,000 has decreased because the prices of goods and services have adjusted due to many variables, from supply chain issues to labor shortages to the massive printing of money. The checks that went out served to hike inflation and then those same checks were taxed at year end without some citizens' knowledge of the "deal" they were getting. Meanwhile, more people came to depend just a little bit more on the government instead of taking responsibility for their own money, finances, and investments wherever possible. The Social Security problem is a similar kind of example, where we are literally stealing from the elderly since the increases in their payments aren't enough to keep up with inflation. For example, even though there have been Cost of Living Adjustments (COLAs) since 1973 on Social Security benefit payouts, the December 2021 COLA of 5.9 percent is likely not going to cover the *real* inflation, which is likely north of 10 percent.

Inflation makes saving look like you're not saving at all, because you aren't. You are slowly losing money to our government's invisible tax.

To summarize: If you save, inflation erodes the value of your money. It's the invisible tax that devalues your money over time, especially if you don't have assets or investments that can hedge against inflation. Inflation therefore tends to affect the poor and middle class heavily. If inflation is very high, in a very short period of time your hard-earned money will be worth very little at all. Weimar Germany is a commonly cited case study to that effect. The government issued money to pay its expenses—a practice that had begun during World War I—but then between 1921 and 1923 the hyperinflation was disastrous to the people and the economy. It was not uncommon to see wheelbarrows of cash brought to buy milk and bread.

So when banks invite you to put money in their vaults, remember, it doesn't just *sit there*. It gets eaten by inflation. It also loses out to the opportunity cost of not investing it.

Thinking back on my own story, what if instead of saving or paying off our zero-interest grace period loan right away we had started our real estate investing *first*? I'll tell you, I'd have a quarter billion in real estate, at least $100 million more working for me.

From the standpoint of control, the choice whether to save, spend, or invest is very much in your hands. Saving doesn't get you a return in the way that the "penny saved, penny earned" attitude would have you believe.

Saving for emergencies and a rainy day is essential, but beyond having that nest egg contingency, saving is really not as great an idea as you might have been taught to think from the vantage point of accruing wealth because it means your money isn't moving. When your money isn't moving, it isn't working for you. *Penny invested, penny earned* is more accurate.

MY BIGGEST MINDSET SHIFT FOR SAVING

I stopped saving so much! In fact, I looked into all the areas where I was saving money and realized I needed to be more aggressive with investing.

If your bank offers you an escrow service on your mortgage, you don't have to accept it.

Instead, tell the bank you'll handle your own taxes and insurance and thanks anyway for their "free" escrow service. Then, for tax and insurance simply set up automatic monthly payments from your savings or checking account to a savings account you set up to hold the escrow payments for the year.

It's not hard and with automation you literally don't have to think about it. I have over one hundred automatic payments moving money from one account to another each month for free. Then the money is there for you to pay your property taxes and insurance at the end of the year but you also get the benefit of collecting interest on your money instead of the bank!

I usually put my escrow funds into a high-yield online savings account and then invest it throughout the year in safe short-term real estate investments, keeping in mind when I'll need the money and how long the investment will run. On the over $1.5 million this year in taxes and insurance I have to pay, I've made about $110,000 by simply automating my escrow versus $0.00 if I had let the bank do it.

Stop giving your own money to the bank to "hold" for you and take advantage of your own money. Every bit of it. While this is a very small example of moving your money, you can apply it to every opportunity you have throughout the year. The concept here is to ensure productivity of every dollar you earn.

PRECEPT #2, REIMAGINED
FOCUS ON INVESTMENTS THAT PAY YOU NOW (INSTEAD OF DIVERSIFYING IN TRADITIONAL INVESTMENTS)

If you think you can understand and control your 401(k), go for it. But if your dream is to avoid working forty to fifty hours per week and then retire around sixty-five, then invest in something that pays you every single month, or at least by the time you're forty.

You simply can't retire on your own terms and in your own time if you are heavily invested in areas you don't understand and control and above all that don't pay you *now*.

In Chapter 1, I asked a few basic questions to challenge your thinking about the 401(k). It was the first investment I learned about and an investment that is *heavily* promoted by society and employers across the board, and so let's really dive into it.

In reality, contributing to a 401(k) immediately presents issues in three categories: (1) automatically giving your money to someone you don't know who puts in into something you don't understand, (2) paying fees you don't understand, and (3) putting dollars into investments you are likely confused about, can't control, and that don't pay you now.

And yet, on my first day of orientation at a Fortune 50, after being told about the many benefits of working for the corporation, I signed over a significant portion of my paycheck every two weeks into a 401(k).

"And not only does that percentage go in tax free, but the company will match 100 percent up to 5 percent," said the company aide, flashing a grin. In other words, if I made $1,000 on a pay stub, I could put $50 of that before taxes into the account, and my employer would also put in $50. The pay stub would read $950. $100 would be added to the 401(k). The company said, you have to do it, it's basically "free" money. But the money is not free; it is in jail.

To this day, my blind decision to fork over money every pay period to an account I barely understood remains one of my worst financial choices, not far behind going into debt to attend college.

Instead, consider this framing: *Every paycheck, we'll take out 5 percent, which you won't see until you're 59.5 years old—if you live that long. If you want to touch and smell your money, you'll have to initiate a two-week cash out process and incur a significant penalty. (Yes, you heard this right, you will pay a penalty to receive your own money back.) If you take out large amounts, you'll also have to be mindful how that affects your end-of-year taxes. Also, please read the fine print for fees to take your money and invest it in index funds that are too complicated for you to understand. Just trust us, it'll be fine most of the time and as long as you keep it with us over many decades, you can ride out the downturns.* (What downturns? Didn't you just say it was a safe investment?)

If a 401(k) had been presented to you that way, would you have signed up for it? Would you continue to contribute to it every paycheck? Would you consider cashing it out and doing something with that money that makes it work harder for you? Do you find it weird that the investment does not allow you to access your own money until you reach a certain age? Are you confused why you are not paying taxes when you put the money in but then paying on the way out?

If you do want to keep your 401(k), consider accessing it to rebalance the investments. Do your research to understand how it is invested, and make informed decisions based on an accurate and complete depiction of the data.

If you want to cash out as an individual, you will often have to provide a destination account some number of days—perhaps ten—in advance of the withdrawal. You'll then be given a summary of the total distribution amount, less federal withholdings. Then, in three or four business days, you will have your distribution. That's a two-week delay in accessing that money, which is probably why standard financial advisors will tell you to hold an emergency fund separate from your 401(k). In an emergency, you wouldn't have the funds in the 401(k) for about two weeks, which is probably too late if you were involved in an actual emergency.

Strictly speaking, the money you've put into a 401(k) is not your money. If your 401(k) is managed by Fidelity, it is rather Fidelity's asset.

But a mediocre financial advisor is not likely to understand this. Instead, they are likely to "educate" you on many of the benefits, without fully laying out the breadth and depth of risks. Again, if they aren't informed themselves, they wouldn't be in a position to advise you on those risks. Meanwhile, if they are incentivized to get you onto a plan, well, you get the idea.

Above all, my biggest beef with the 401(k)s is that they don't pay us *now*. They pay you at a time that may not align with your vision for life and Financial Freedom and that you should be taking into serious consideration.

Instead of diversifying in traditional investments, focus on investments that pay you now.

MY BIGGEST MINDSET SHIFT FOR INVESTMENTS

This was pretty easy for me. My learning was to stop putting my money in this investment, the 401(k). I didn't need money when I was sixty; I wanted money when I was forty-five, so this investment was like putting my money in jail and not having access to it until too late in life for my goals. Even though I didn't know where to put it yet, I knew it couldn't be here...and I needed to continue to look into and try other investments that aligned with my vision.

Keep this simple. If your goal is Financial Freedom before sixty, the 401(k)s, Roth IRAs, and many other traditional investments you've been told about just don't align with your vision and shouldn't be invested in.

PRECEPT #3, REIMAGINED
EVALUATE ANY ADVICE YOU RECEIVE, EVEN FROM YOUR FINANCIAL ADVISOR

Have you ever had an experience with a financial advisor where you felt they weren't advising you on your choice but rather directing you toward certain options? This is a red flag. Now, to be fair, the system at times puts financial advisors in this position with incentives that don't align with yours. When this occurs, you can ask questions to find alignment. For example, if you're being guided toward a 401(k), stocks, and mutual funds, you could ask if there are additional investment opportunities to discuss.

When I consider taking advice, I am interested in whether I can ascertain the level of understanding the advice giver has. If someone has made their name as an actor, do I really want to give them credit for their political opinions? Short of providing a well-reasoned argument, the success rate of the messenger in the domain of expertise at hand does matter. But even then, the quality of the reasoning—the message—matters most of all. It's up to you to evaluate it.

When it comes to stockbrokers or life insurance salespeople or financial advisors, apply the same standards. If a financial advisor suggests things like riding out the 20 percent dip, keeping savings in the bank, and sticking with your diversified and "safe" investments long term to take advantage of compounding interest, ask *Why?* If their response is, "Because I'm a financial advisor," you may have to keep looking for a financial advisor.

If you do have someone working with you who knows their stuff, the next step is to understand their motivations. For instance, have you ever been offered a contract by a financial institution or advisor in which that institution or advisor has skin in the game to the point that they will participate in *your* downside?

It only seems reasonable, to me anyway, that if they are going to give you such confident advice they should accept some responsibility when that advice does not work out in your favor. That would be a win–win instead of a win–lose relationship.

When I played basketball, and I didn't perform, my coach took me out of the game. That was fair and effective. If I played well, putting up good numbers and supporting my teammates, I got more minutes.

And, yet, most agreements will dictate that your financial advisor still pockets a management fee regardless of your success or failure.

But even before we get there, consider the following: How often have you calculated what they are costing you?

I'm not just talking about all the fees. I'm talking about the returns. How much is working with a financial advisor *costing* you? Do you understand their financial capabilities or do you take that for granted because they are called a financial advisor and your friend recommended them? What makes someone qualified?

Assuming you know your financial advisor, working with him or her still plays into two categories: paying fees you do not understand and making investments you do not understand.

Seeing as we are talking about literacy, wouldn't it make sense to have a better financial literacy baseline before reaching out to someone? Wouldn't it be sound due diligence to find out whether the financial advisors you approach are actually wealthy themselves (and how they did it)? Wouldn't it be reasonable to spend some time figuring out if your potential financial advisor understands your vision and how you want to invest to align with that vision? If not, you'll have to assess what to do when you see those red flags. Don't be afraid of changing your financial advisor or challenging them to provide you more value, but do yourself a favor and do your own homework first. Consider asking your financial advisor questions like: When do you want to be financially free? What's your net worth? How are you planning on reaching Financial Freedom?

You may be tired, feel uneducated, or even feel it is unnecessary to become financially literate. Well, unfortunately, I need to be honest with you...you don't have time *not* to learn. Don't outsource your foundational understanding. At least not in the beginning. You need to get educated and you need to get interested in money and how it works. If you don't, the odds are much smaller that you'll reach Financial Freedom. So take a minute to change your mindset. This isn't a want, this is a need. Start slow, but *start*. If someone never tries to learn the alphabet, how can they ever learn to read?

MY BIGGEST MINDSET SHIFT FOR FINANCIAL ADVISORS

I learned that my financial advisor wasn't as wealthy as I wanted to be, didn't have the same goals, and was in a job where he had to continue trading his time to make more money. When my wife and I brought our Financial Freedom goal of forty-five years to our financial advisor, unfortunately he both tried to dissuade us from that approach and continued attempting to persuade us to play it safe with our money.

That resistance, from the very person I hoped to be able to speak most openly about my financial plans with, led us to part ways with our financial advisor. And yet I hope you've understood that I'm not asking you to do that. I've only provided a few questions to help you check that you and your financial advisor are a great fit for each other. And I want to stress, you can and should outsource a lot of things in your life, like cleaning your house, but completely outsourcing your financial literacy is not one of those things.

Having made this decision left me worried for a while, since I still didn't understand where I would put my money...but I did know I needed to make it more productive. We didn't give up.

PRECEPT #4, REIMAGINED

MAKE YOUR MONEY PRODUCTIVE

Debt should not be feared, it should be understood. When it is understood you can make it more productive.

It's a mistake to only look at the cost of debt. That's leaving out the other half of the equation: its impact on cash flow. If I take out a loan on the Tesla I already own outright and those funds bring in revenue faster than the cost of the loan repayment, I come out ahead.

In other words, taking on debt can be an opportunity to invest. Can you invest it in a low-risk way for better yields? Answering that question puts a new spin on anxiety-driving and possibly misplaced goals like paying off a fifteen-year home mortgage early. If a fifteen-year mortgage is at 2.75 percent, it only makes sense to pay off that mortgage early if you don't have a way to make at least 3 percent on that same money through an investment.

What about other kinds of debt? Student loans are a big one. They are a very tricky subject because there is a lot of attention on them at the moment. Combined with the rising costs of university education, student loans have crippled people and made it difficult for them to escape. Until recently the idea of declaring bankruptcy wasn't even on the table. Businesses can declare bankruptcy, but individuals were saddled with that debt indefinitely. Today, I'd be very wary of taking on any student debts, even though that's what I did only a decade ago.

Each kind of debt will have a certain term and interest rate associated. Credit cards tend to come with high interest rates, which is why it is sound advice to pay them off in a timely manner. The same can't be said for car loans. Maybe your loan has a decent interest rate of about 2 percent. Maybe you are in a good cash position and you have the opportunity to pay that off and avoid paying future interest. Should you do it? That depends. If at the same time you could invest that same money and get a 6 percent return, you'd come out 4 percent ahead by continuing to pay the monthly payments for the remainder of the loan period.

When you consider both the cost of debt *and* the cash flow potential of a low risk investment of that debt, only then are you fully embracing the productivity of money.

MY BIGGEST MINDSET SHIFT FOR MAKING MONEY PRODUCTIVE

I put down 35 percent on the first home when I should have put down only around 25 percent. To mitigate that mistake I took out a home equity line of credit (HELOC), essentially a second mortgage, and used the equity I pulled out of the first property to buy another property. The beauty of this move was that the second property was now effectively paying off that second mortgage and most of the first mortgage too (the HELOC).

In summary, I both stopped paying down my home faster and I also used the HELOC to buy a duplex that has a 20 percent ConC return. This duplex not only paid the increase in mortgage but ended up paying the entire mortgage for me. That was a game changer as I used more debt to create more cash flow and therefore that increase in expense each month on the debt was worth it because the increase in income it allowed me to bring in was much larger.

THE TRIFECTA OF INVESTMENTS

The best investments are those which:

- You understand.
- You can control.
- Pay you *now*.

Combined with my key learnings, my view of money and how I deployed it shifted dramatically once I became interested in understanding how money works in our current system. When I found an investment I could understand and control, and that paid me now, I was well on my way to Financial Freedom. It was challenging to level with myself that I'd been wrong about money and investments for my entire life. But I was also invigorated by the opportunity to look at money differently, to take charge, and to seek better and better ways to make my money work for me.

When you understand, control, and are getting paid *now*, you can passively add cash flow month over month. That's powerful.

When I got into real estate, I knew that I didn't know much. I didn't know how to fix a washing machine. But in the first month when the washing machine broke at the house, I looked up an online video, got the tools, and learned. I also didn't know how to make improvements to my properties. I also didn't know how to creatively finance larger purchases. But knowing that I didn't know these things let me further explore them, and ultimately scale. That scale was what sped up our trajectory toward Financial Freedom. That's how we got there at age thirty instead of age forty-five like we initially planned.

YOUR PROGRESS REPORT
TOWARD FINANCIAL FREEDOM

1. *Honestly challenge norms and beliefs.* ✔
2. *Decide what Financial Freedom is to you, when you want it, and with what intensity level.* ✔
3. *Define and boot up the systems to run your life like a CEO.* ✔
4. *Light up your scoreboard.* ✔
5. *Become financially literate.* ✔
6. Learn how to scale.
7. Teach your sons and daughters to fish.
8. See how I built my real estate business.

The Three-Step Financial Freedom Process:
1. *Set a vision for your life.* ✔
2. *Through awareness and sacrifice, organize your life to increase cash flow with your time.* ✔
3. *Invest your money in assets that increase your cash flow.* ✔

CHAPTER 6

SCALE

"Give me a lever long enough, and a place
to stand, and I will move the earth."
—ARCHIMEDES, MATHEMATICIAN

Undoubtedly, I get asked the most, How did you scale so fast? How did you go from $40,000 in debt in 2010 to Financial Freedom in 2017, at thirty years of age? How did you go from $40,000 in debt to hitting $1 million in just seven years? And then, in only a few years after that, how did you go from seven to eight digits in net worth?

I built a property management business from five employees to fifty, from a payroll of $96,000 in 2019 to wrapping up this last year (2021) at $1.5 million in payroll, from gross revenue of $625,000 to over $13 million. All in two years.

I bought my first rental property back in 2013 and ended the year with $85,000 worth of real estate investments. Today, I own over $150 million in real estate and more than 1,500 rental units. I know a little something about scaling. It's not easy. Growth comes with risk, comes with big problems, lots of change. But here's the deal: I've taught you most of these secrets already. And if you really want to scale, buckle up, because I'm going to put them all together.

STAY FOCUSED ON THE VISION

If you want to scale, you must be disciplined in the three-step process that I've shared, think and understand opportunity costs, and really educate yourself when it comes to velocity of money and the productivity of your money. The Netflix and chill nights are over. The work and build nights are ahead.

This means understanding and developing effective repeatable processes. Learn how to take these simple systems and make them work for you. If done well and if done with discipline, you can achieve outstanding results. The problem that most encounter is that they don't continue to repeat the process. Most don't evolve. Most don't stay disciplined with the process.

Here's the short version of how I scaled. Hopefully some of this sounds familiar from Chapters 2, 3, and 4.

I truly live and breathe my ultimate vision. I take time to slow down to understand what I want most. So at one time it was Financial Freedom. Now, I wouldn't just reveal my ultimate vision and my intensity level once a month, I would truly live and breathe it. I'm talking about putting what I really want on the mirror, in the car, on my phone. I visualize this goal. I live this goal. I breathe this goal. It was ingrained into my mindset, into my decisions, into the opportunities that I had in front of me. This is really, really important because we make tons of micro decisions every single day. And if you want to scale, then you've got to *focus*. And if you focus, you've got to focus on what matters most.

Then, I quickly got real with my cash flow. I made choices that some thought were tough, like sticking with an old car, eating peanut butter and jelly sandwiches, living in a small home that we were outgrowing, and rarely going on vacations and choosing budget-conscious options when we did. A lot of people would say those decisions were tough.

When I look back, those were sacrifices, but they were small sacrifices compared to what so many people, including myself, were giving up to not achieve their ultimate goal. Despite my sacrifices, I was not scaling at the speed I wanted in order to achieve Financial Freedom or other things in life.

So you see, this second step, where you analyze how much you are making and how much you are spending, is about, *Do you truly want to scale?* Because scaling is about speed. Scaling is about the pace and it is okay if you want to scale slowly, but make sure you understand that you are making decisions—conscious decisions, not unconscious ones—to be aware. And for me, if you're asking how I scaled so fast in so many different things in my life right here, it's this step: I visualized what I wanted and involved that visualization in every decision.

I think the biggest thing I want to hit on here, though, is expenses. A lot of people think that we were tough, that we were making difficult sacrifices, but managing expenses is actually the easy part. Just focus on what matters and say no to everything else that gets in your way. Because that's ultimately what you want.

Then income. On my journey, I didn't have much. I was not only $40,000 in debt, but I also wasn't making very much money when I started out. But I had a choice. And I think you have a choice. If you hate your job and you want to scale, I highly recommend quitting your job and finding something that you like, because ultimately in this journey, the more income that you are going to make is going to help you create more money to invest. And if you have a job that you hate, ultimately it's going to be really, really hard to continue to make more money because you won't be as passionate about it. Fortunately, for me on my scaling journey, I *did* like my job. And because I didn't make very much money, I decided to work harder at it.

That's what I recommend to you as well. If you like your job, double down on your effort. In my case, I didn't just read personal finance books or real estate books. I started reading leadership books because I was a leader at a Fortune 50 company and I wanted to produce better results so that I could provide more value for my company. And that's exactly what I did. And that's how I was able to promote a half dozen times over the course of a decade and make more and more and more money.

I think this is key because some people get distracted when they're trying to scale. Some people start paying more attention to their investments and not paying enough attention to their job. It can feel like a juggling act but you don't want to let any ball drop. You can't afford not to keep your eyes on all the balls in the air. You do need more income because you can only cut so many expenses. Just like I've talked about in previous chapters, cutting expenses is finite; making more income is, by contrast, relatively infinite. So if you spend more time and effort and actually focus on making more money at your job, then if you have a job that you like at a company that rewards performance, like I did, you will continue to make more and more money.

So as I started to make more and more money by doubling down on my job and getting promoted, I also paid closer attention to really ensure that my hard work was put into invest-ments that then worked hard for me. This is the tough part with scaling. You can't just visualize it. You can't just work really hard. You can't just make sacrifices. You also have to educate the mind. You've got to read. You've got to grow. I started reading books. As I shared in previous chapters, I would start reading one book a month to educate myself on investments and how to truly put my money to work. I didn't need a mentor. I didn't need a finan-cial advisor. What I needed to do was *evolve* my mind. And for-tunately in today's world, between books, podcasts, and search engines, there is so much out there that can help you grasp the fundamentals. And sometimes, it takes first understanding what's *not* going to help you with your goal.

I tried a 401(k), I tried stocks and other things, and a lot of these investments didn't help me scale because they don't pay me *today*. If you want to scale, you need velocity. You need to velocitize your money, which means investing in vehicles that give you frequent returns. That means taking your hard-earned money, putting it in an investment, and that investment gives you money now. Take that money and put it back into the investment or a new investment. The cycle continues and you start to stack.

For me, a lot of my goals centered around the investment of real estate. Real estate is a huge catalyst for scaling because it does pay you now as recurring cash flow every single month.

And as I educated myself and as I changed my mindset, and as I started to understand real estate more and more, I started to realize that the more money I could invest in real estate, the more money I would get back. And the more money I would get back would give me more money to be able to put back in real estate, which would create this cycle of velocity.

I WENT BROKE OVER AND OVER AND OVER AGAIN

I need my money to work hard. I need it to be productive. I need that money now so that I can continue to move the wheel faster and faster. And then I did something that I think most people are too scared to do, or most people see as too uncomfortable or too much of a risk: I went broke over and over and over again.

Even though at this point I'd been getting promoted and was making over six digits, I was spending very little because I knew I wanted to scale. I knew my vision. And crucially now, finally I *knew* that investment—I educated myself and I was understanding real estate more and more and more. Then I went broke. This means I would take all the money I had and I'd buy another investment property because I knew that with that money, I only had three choices: I could spend it, I could save it, or I could invest it. If I spent it, that money was gone. If I saved it, I was losing to inflation and the opportunity cost of not investing. So, as quick as possible and as much as possible, I would get that money back into investments like real estate.

It became a game. How much money can I make in a month? And how much of that money that I made can I get into real estate? I loved not having money. I was making a lot of money, but I didn't have the money. And I started to love the process. In fact, where most people say they're burning a hole in their

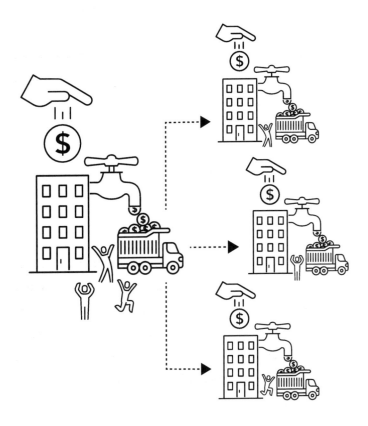

pocket to spend, for me, anytime I had money it was burning a hole in my pocket to *invest*. I didn't want the money. I didn't want my bank account to say $1 million in savings. I wanted it to say $1 in savings. I really want to emphasize that because to scale you've got to go all in. And I was all in.

In everything, if you visualize and you want it bad enough, and you want it quick enough and you have the intensity high enough, then you're going to do everything you possibly can to achieve that in the shortest time period possible.

There's only one way to do that. You're going to take all the chips that you're making and plow them in so that you have no chips left over. There is no safety net. You need to put it all in. Then you measure it. You continue stacking, you continue investing, and you continue to measure your scoreboard. Is it heading in the right direction?

RISK MITIGATION

To have the confidence to make big bets, it is helpful to feel secure when it comes to your basic survival: your expenses and an emergency fund. Through awareness and the cash flow reviews, I know exactly what my expenses are and how much cash I need to cover them. Additionally, I ensure that I set aside the minimum for an emergency fund as well.

CREATING OPTIONS

Then something very interesting happens because you're getting so much money back now and it's velocitizing. You're not just taking your hard-earned money every single month and buying investments. You're taking your hard-earned money plus the money that your investments are now making. You and your assets actually start to buy investments alongside you. So that's when I could feel the speed really start because before my assets started buying more assets, I was the only vehicle to buy these real estate investments. But now my real estate investments are buying real estate investments. That's velocity.

When I started velocitizing, we made more and more money. Our assets were buying assets. Our cash flow was increasing. Our net worth was increasing. My W-2 job was productive. I was still working seventy hours a week, traveling out of state for three to five days a week across the United States. The results for my employer were also strong and I came up for promotion. I was told that even though I'd delivered results and fulfilled the role's responsibilities, often going beyond them, the only way to get this next promotion was to relocate. It sounded so simple. So easy. But that's a big ask, isn't it? How easy is it to uproot your entire family? Find a new place to live, kids in a new school, the time to settle into a new city.

I remember expressing, "I just spent a year and a half on the road, away from my family. You know I just had my second child. My results not only met expectations, they exceeded them consistently. I received the very top score every year during reviews."

We both knew that hadn't happened without a lot of hard work, a lot of sacrifices, and a lot of results. That's why the company continued to promote me and I was very thankful for those promotions.

This particular promotion was one I'd seen people *beg* for. I'd seen people work twice as long as I'd worked. This was a promotion and a job that I knew a ton of people had taken and wanted...but I realized for the first time I didn't want it.

I want to emphasize something. Up to that point, I loved my career. I embraced being a leader. I derived meaning from impacting lives. I enjoyed driving operations, producing results for my company. And my company had continued to pay me more and more and give me more responsibility to keep me engaged, to help my brain continue to evolve.

I didn't even give a second thought to saying yes to past promotions. But now, for the first time, I realized that my focus on productivity and velocity of my money had created the real estate investment on the side. Because of that, I realized for the first time that I was in a position of power. I politely said, "I need time to think about it."

That Saturday, I remember looking at what I'd scaled. And at that time I had scaled to about 180 units. And while the company was paying me a great salary, my 180 units on *ten hours a month* of my time versus the *ten hours a day* of W-2 time was producing the same amount of money.

Remember, folks, it's not about what you make. It's about what you keep. And I was in the highest tax bracket with my W-2 leadership job. But in the real estate business, I was building my 180 to 200 units and I wasn't paying anything for taxes. So in *ten hours a month versus ten hours a day*, I was making the same amount in my real estate. And it occurred to me that my employer was not in a position of power anymore. I was. A thought occurred to me. I don't have to move. I don't have to take this promotion. I don't even have to work for this company anymore if I don't like it, if I don't enjoy it. And I don't appreciate being put in the position that I was.

I made the decision that weekend to investigate how much more I could make if I increased the amount of time I was spending on real estate investing. I realized that now I had options, thanks to the cash flow real estate was providing. It was up to me whether to exercise those options. In particular, I had the option not to work a W-2 job anymore, and set my sights on the most opportune time to go all in on the real estate business. Maybe you too will see that as you begin moving toward Financial Freedom that you have the option to choose to do more of what you enjoy across several domains in your life.

VELOCITY

If you stay disciplined, it's crazy how fast you can stack. It's crazy how fast you can scale. And it's crazy how fast you may be able to put yourself in a position of power. Whether you liked your job in the past, one thing is for sure: things change, things evolve, and you will need to put yourself in a position to have *options*.

To scale, it takes moving all your money into these investments that pay you now, investments that you can control, investments that you understand, combined with a continued thirst to grow and evolve your mindset.

As you accomplish these things, your scoreboard really starts to light up. It starts to get easier.

To wrap up this chapter, I want to share a secret with you. And the secret is, you have got to move the money. Moving money is everything to scale. And I think I've shared with you throughout this chapter how I did. As fast as you get the money, you've got to move it into that investment. The speed at which you can move money will produce higher and higher returns. And don't forget when that money is sitting, when you are choosing to leave that money in the bank, in your 401(k), even in your house, when you're choosing to spend that money and not putting it into an investment, there's an opportunity cost.

the secret is that money has got to move. I didn't understand that right away. And it slowed everything down in my
journey. I would do dumb things like pay off a 2.77 percent
mortgage faster on my house. I didn't do Step One or Step
Three in this case, because Step One is understanding your goals
of being financially free, and paying off your house does nothing
for Financial Freedom, because that produces no real income.
And Step Three assesses the productivity of your money, of
how hard your money is working for you. And by paying off
my house, the speed of my money, the returns of my money was
simply a 2.77 percent return, less than inflation, a terrible decision. You need to do all three steps and you have to continue to
put all three steps in the forefront of your mind. Step Three is
obviously essential.

Once you find that investment like I did with real estate,
learn everything you can about it and keep pushing all the chips
in. I scaled quickly because I understand the process. I live and
breathe the process.

- Number one. My vision is clear. I know what I'm after.
And I focus on it. And I focus on that thing more than
anything else. Do you?

- Number two. I keep organized. I keep organized and I'm
aware of my cash flow monthly. Are you?

- Number three. I continue to educate myself to learn about money and to invest as much as I can in the investments that are the highest productivity. Do you?

But most people do this:

- One. They don't take time to have a vision. Their vision is not clear. Therefore they make small micro decisions on a daily, weekly, monthly basis that lead them astray.

- Two. Most people aren't organized and aren't aware of their monthly cash flow. Therefore, without consciously knowing they are sacrificing what they ultimately want in life.

- Three. A lot of people are too tired, or a lot of people don't educate themselves on money or on the thing that they want the most. Instead, they rely on unreliable people, advisors, etc., that steer them away from making their own decisions and being accountable to them.

If you're like most people, don't let it get you down. Starting today you can become unusual in a good way.

YOUR PROGRESS REPORT
TOWARD FINANCIAL FREEDOM

1. *Honestly challenge norms and beliefs.* ✔
2. *Decide what Financial Freedom is to you, when you want it, and with what intensity level.* ✔
3. *Define and boot up the systems to run your life like a CEO.* ✔
4. *Light up your scoreboard.* ✔
5. *Become financially literate.* ✔
6. *Learn how to scale.* ✔
7. Teach your sons and daughters to fish.
8. See how I built my real estate business.

The Three-Step Financial Freedom Process:
1. Set a vision for your life. ✔
2. Through awareness and sacrifice, organize your life to increase cash flow with your time. ✔
3. Invest your money in assets that increase your cash flow. ✔

.

CHAPTER 7

LEGACY

....

*"Tell me and I forget. Teach me and I
remember. Involve me and I learn."*

—BENJAMIN FRANKLIN,
WRITER, SCIENTIST, INVENTOR

————————————————

have the best parents ever. Growing up, they loved me and
supported me. And they taught me so much. But one thing
they did not teach me is how money works. Probably because
they were not taught. As a result, we simply didn't talk about

money. If you don't even talk about something, how can you learn about it, much less become experienced?

To break this cycle, what if you not only talked about money with your children, but also did activities with them? People may be afraid to talk about money, but that fear can be overcome knowing that by discussing money and by giving your children decision-making experiences, you are giving a great gift to the next generation.

Don't wait for someone else to do this. Don't wait for them to learn poor habits from their friends. Don't wait for the government to teach your kids through public education. It is a good step to review your child's school curriculum—see what classes they are taking and what books are being presented to your kids—and maybe even coordinate with other moms and dads to work for changes in that curriculum. What if your children could be taught about money and logical decision-making in school? But if the school isn't fast to change, you don't have to wait. Teach your children what they need to learn.

I wrote this book because there weren't people around me to learn from growing up. Sometimes wealthy families teach their kids by involving them in the family business or through dinner-table conversations. But not all of them. When it comes to families that aren't wealthy, it's often the case that mothers and fathers didn't have the education themselves, so they can't easily impart wisdom about money to their children. Sometimes they are learning right alongside their kids.

Even high schools and colleges in general are not actively teaching students how to think about money or providing exercises in basic logic. But why wait until high school or college, anyway? Your children might be way behind by then. Maybe the activities in this chapter will let your children get a head start on thinking about money, making decisions, and making money work for them. If you come from a family where money lessons were lacking, then this may just be the beginning of a fresh start and the seeds of generational learning to come.

VISION FOR KIDS

My son is seven years of age and he wants to buy a car. Now, around age seven or eight is when kids begin developing the ability to use logic, whereas before they rely on Mom and Dad to help them understand the meaning of things. I don't know how long my son's vision will include that car, but maybe this presents a learning moment.

The interesting thing about that vision is that the car is expensive, but he also has a lot of time to get the money since he won't have his driver's license for another nine years. Meanwhile, if we set a routine to periodically check in on this vision, it's possible other goals will come into focus as well.

VISION ACTIVITY

Ask your son or daughter what they want, by when, and with what level of intensity. Sound familiar? Sit with them and present those questions one at a time. After completing the exercise, review their responses together. Are they happy with them? Ask, What did you learn about yourself having answered those questions? Save their responses for review next month.

If your son or daughter is already a teenager, these questions may be a little more difficult, but perhaps even more rewarding. Maybe your teenager will realize that a part of their vision involves an activity that requires detailed sustained effort or a small business that requires their dedication and money management. Of course, setting the vision is only step one.

CASH FLOW BUDGET FOR KIDS

There are a variety of strategies I've heard about that moms and dads use to get their kids used to making decisions about money. One I've come across is a weekly or monthly allowance. Another common one is chores around the house. Once the kids get the money through the allowance or the chores, they get to decide how to use it. This is actually a great way to introduce children to the concept of money.

But what if you took it a step further? How can we introduce children to the concept of the cash flow budget? If we could, then they would understand both income and expenses and be exposed to the ideas of net cash flow. Your net cash flow is only positive if your income is greater than your expenses for a given time period.

What may not be as useful are toys like a piggy bank or money jar. The reason being that these tend to help kids objectify money and incentivize accumulation instead of develop a responsible relationship with money. Piggy banks and money jars keep money standing still and inaccessible.

CASH FLOW BUDGET ACTIVITY

Every thirty days, sit with your children to review their income and expenses. Maybe you are providing them with an allowance of $20 a month. Obviously that goes in the income column. What expenses do they have? Maybe you could charge them $5 a month in "rent." That leaves a net of $15, *if* they didn't spend any of that money. Have your children list out what they spent their money on that month and calculate the cash flow.

After listing income and expenses and calculating the net cash flow, predict the next month's cash flow.

Talk through each line item. This not only helps your children with wants versus needs but also helps them explore ways to increase their income. Are there additional chores they'd like to take on around the house? If they are older, are there odd jobs or businesses they could start in the neighborhood or online?

Really slow down and have the "intensity" conversation with them. How bad do they want it? That should determine their effort for trading their time for more money.

INVESTMENTS FOR KIDS

You might be thinking, How can I teach my kids about investments when I have only just started to learn? We're going to start small. It's less about what is right or wrong and more about the decision-making process. Your children will learn through those decisions and reflecting on those decisions.

The key when it comes to investments is this: instead of trading time for money (as with chores), what if money could be used to make more money? As you remind your child about their vision and as they hopefully start to accumulate more money towards that vision goal, this will open the door for an opportunity to teach the final step...what to do with that money they have traded their time for and made sacrifices for too.

INVESTMENTS ACTIVITY

If your son or daughter wants to earn money, have them buy all the materials to make candy treats. For example, say you want to make candy pretzels. Take your son or daughter to the store. Walk through the store, collect the materials, and make your way to the register. Have your son or daughter pay the cashier with paper money so that they experience exchanging it for the materials. (I could see the sadness on my son's face when the money was gone.)

At home, it's time to get to work. But before you do, establish a figure you'd like to hit in terms of returns. If materials cost $30, maybe you try to double that for $60. How many treats do you need to make? How much should you sell them for? How will you market them? Will you deliver them to neighbors by knocking on doors or sell them through a group online?

My son ended up selling all 60 of his candy pretzels at $1 per pretzel and ended up with a net gain of $30 for his efforts. He learned how much effort, and how much fun, it was to buy, make, and sell the pretzels. He had earned it and the smile on his face said it all. Then during the monthly financial plan review with your son or daughter, add this to the cash flow. For my son, seeing how before he was averaging $15 a month ($5 for rent and $20 for chores), and from this investment of his money he now made $30 net, was really impactful. It was also impactful having the conversation with him about seeing that his expenses went up to $35 that month but, more importantly, his income went up to $80. I would encourage you to then discuss "time" with your kid. The $30 net was two months worth of trading his time for money ($15 net per month).

Admittedly, this candy selling example taught my son a few things about business. It didn't, however, yet teach him about scalable investments and this business idea traded more of his time with money.

SCALE FOR KIDS

Scaling requires that money be made to work even harder for you, with limited trading of your own time.

My son recently bought a coin-operated washer and dryer in the basement of one of my apartments from me for $100 each. Now, for a young person that may be a sizable investment in terms of upfront cost. However, now the washer and dryer units collect quarters from customers doing their laundry. All my son has to do is visit the apartments to collect the revenue and ensure the units are operating as designed.

Similarly, my son bought a candy-dispensing machine in an office building. Same principle. Upfront investment and some expenses to replace the purchased candy. But the effort is minimal compared with the one-time sale candy pretzels. My son visits the office building once a month to pick up his quarters. Compared to doing chores, stopping by the office is a pretty good deal. Plus, he likes the idea of treating himself to the candy if the profits are good that month!

SCALE ACTIVITY

If your son or daughter is beginning to create medium- or longer-term visions, it may be a great time to talk about scale. Probably by now, too, they are more accurately predicting the results of their cash flow budget.

At the end of a monthly review, tack on these questions: How could you reach your goals sooner? How could you increase your cash flow month over month? What other options do you have?

For example, my son would never be able to buy a car on his own at $15 net profit per month. So eventually he will need to learn how to increase cash flow. The business idea was great, but again, that means trading more time, which does increase cash flow but requires considerable effort. He will have to come up with something else. Maybe instead of the laundry machines, I could have helped my son by asking him how to sell pretzels with less of his time? How? He would have paid his sister to help make and sell them. This is great because most people want to do *everything* themselves and are focused only on the expenses. But remember, it is about cash flow. Expenses are only 5 percent of your energy here...so helping him realize he could make twice the output and realize the expense of his sister's labor would be an awesome realization at an early age.

Here's a chance to really think bigger and more long term. With a few months or years of practice in setting their vision and keeping a cash flow budget, they will be ready to test themselves to reach those goals even faster using their innate creativity and desire to explore. The ideas they come up with may be in this book or beyond it. It is our responsibility as parents to guide young children, but as they mature, they may see possibilities previous generations haven't seen. Let them run with it!

SEIZE AND ENJOY THIS RESPONSIBILITY

Schools are not giving kids $10 for doing their homework and then using that $10 to teach kids how to make these decisions. So it is actually the responsibility of mothers and fathers or whoever is taking care of them to offer that educational opportunity at the end of the day. If they don't learn it then, they will learn it later, probably in the form of a mistake that takes additional time and effort to correct. You can save them this pain by having them do the exercises above, or even create your own! What a gift and legacy that could turn out to be.

That's much different than how my childhood was when it came to money. Because I wasn't taught to ask questions. Instead, I was given rules. *Save money. Reduce debt. Invest in a 401(k).*

Going forward, our sons and daughters will know how to ask questions. Will be unafraid to ask them. Will step up and inquire. Will activate their curiosity. Will listen to each other and investigate the data. If there is no data to be had, they will tread lightly until they learn more.

Learning to ask questions, to challenge one's own thinking and beliefs, and that of others, is one of the biggest superpowers available today.

Of course, you can run an internet search on almost any topic. But the searches are only as good as the questions you put in. Your discernment will help you decide what is worth investigating to begin with. Then your intent will guide you toward good applications of your newfound knowledge.

When I reflect on my journey, it was when I realized that I could think for myself and explore things that I really started to change my path. That wasn't until my twenties. What if kids were shown this much earlier in life?

Being able to think critically, or simply the ability to think in general, should be at the core of any education. This does not require tens of thousands of dollars (nor hundreds of thousands at the university level). So, I don't worry too much about saving money to help pay my kids' way through college. Let's see if college is even still a thing society expects of young adults in a few years. I am not putting money on it, which is why I'm betting that the activities above, or your variations of them, might much better serve your children than a 529 plan putting away money for college. A 529 plan is another example of an investment that keeps your money still and which you don't have control over. So if you shouldn't invest in it, why would you invest in it for your kids?

In my son and daughter's case, we've already bought an investment property that will go into their name at age eighteen. At that time, they will have the chance to decide how to proceed. Will they keep the cash-flow-positive investment? Will they sell it to help them start a business or go to college? Something else? That will be up to them. The practice they've had up until then will be their preparation for those decisions. And you better believe, I have them helping run the investment properties right now.

YOUR PROGRESS REPORT
TOWARD FINANCIAL FREEDOM

1. *Honestly challenge norms and beliefs.* ✔
2. *Decide what Financial Freedom is to you, when you want it, and with what intensity level.* ✔
3. *Define and boot up the systems to run your life like a CEO.* ✔
4. *Light up your scoreboard.* ✔
5. *Become financially literate.* ✔
6. *Learn how to scale.* ✔
7. *Teach your sons and daughters to fish.* ✔
8. See how I built my real estate business.

The Three-Step Financial Freedom Process:
1. *Set a vision for your life.* ✔
2. *Through awareness and sacrifice, organize your life to increase cash flow with your time.* ✔
3. *Invest your money in assets that increase your cash flow.* ✔

REAL ESTATE

"Real estate isn't the asset—what you do to create value for others through real estate is the asset, and a valid path to prosperity."

—GARRETT B. GUNDERSON, AUTHOR

Real estate has everything I look for in an investment: understanding, control, and cash flow now.

If you've even considered trying real estate investing, but you haven't yet tried it, why haven't you?

Let me be up front with you—I want you to try real estate. This chapter is going to explore my very first deal and list out every major benefit I've enjoyed from real estate investing. I'll even share a few mistakes I made so that you can skip right over them. Even though I've been doing real estate investing since 2013, I feel this is just the beginning. In future books I'm hoping to share lessons learned operating and repositioning real estate with actual examples so that you can get excited and have as much fun as we are having with this type of investment. The benefits of real estate are rarely if at all talked about in school, in society, and with financial advisors.

Recently, my sister and brother-in-law, a social worker and a police officer, came to me and admitted they should have gotten into real estate sooner, probably five years ago when I was enthusiastically trying to get them started. They realized what I was talking about was starting to work for them and they saw the potential. Yes, they probably should have started sooner, but that's in the past: I'm excited for them to go on this journey. Real estate is not only for the wealthy, smart, and connected. It can be for anyone. A twenty-eight-year-old I coached went from no knowledge and no properties to over one hundred in two years. And I know plenty of multimillionaires in this space who didn't even make it through high school.

As I've shared, when it came to choosing investments, I tried the 401(k) and I tried the Roth IRA. I tried mutual funds and stocks. You name it, I've tried it. But none of them truly offered me what I needed from an investment to align with my vision. There are certain questions that you have to ask yourself that you don't even need a financial advisor to ask.

Do I understand where my money is exactly? Can I forecast my returns accurately? Do I have control of it? Does the investment pay me now (monthly or at least this year)? Do I have an idea of how to make it even more productive? Do I understand the fees, the taxes, the inflation, or anything else that cuts into my returns? Truly take time to look at these questions. These are for you to answer. Not your financial advisor. But heck, for fun, maybe ask your financial advisor too.

DID YOU KNOW?

Did you know that 87 percent of the wealthiest people have real estate investments? If you have an advisor, do they own real estate? Have they offered real estate as an investment? If they haven't, why haven't they, if this high of a percentage of wealthy people do have it? Have you considered why financial advisors don't? Have you considered why you haven't tried it yet?

When I went through my investment opportunities, I just wasn't getting the productivity I wanted. The potential of real estate stood out and the opportunity soon came to us. We seized it.

In this chapter I'll use my first investment to illustrate several benefits and then expand from there. I've found that starting small is approachable. Even if you've already invested in a few properties, getting access to how I approach a real estate deal, my overall investment style, and my plans for the future may help you as well.

PREPPING FOR THE FIRST DEAL

When I started considering real estate, my wife and I didn't know anything or anyone in this space. It's not like we had a mentor. It's not like we had some rich friend or relative. In fact, I have coached over 200 people who started with no real estate get into real estate and grow their portfolios rather quickly. So if you are like I was, knowing nothing about real estate, don't be afraid. Entrepreneur Farshad Asl said, "When your ambition is greater than your fear, your life will get bigger than your dream."

I learned most of what I know through books from people who actually invested in real estate—not from people who only teach it. Then I applied what I learned and gained experience. You can do this too.

I want to give you a real example to learn from. The numbers that follow are "based on a true story." One day you may have 100 or even 1,000 units, but the journey to 1,000 starts with a single unit; at least it did for me.

I sought the answer to the basic investment questions: (1) Do I understand this investment?, (2) Can I control it?, and (3) Is it predictable and can I make it more productive over time?

DO I UNDERSTAND?

Unlike reading report after annual report on companies where I was investing my stocks (and trying to understand what that company is going to do in the next year), real estate investment property is much simpler. A building just has four walls. You can see it. You can even feel it. It is not as complicated and scary as you may think. As I started to educate myself, I realized that understanding a property is so much easier than understanding a lot of other investments. And maybe this is just me, but there's something about *seeing* that investment that gave me a better understanding of how things worked. That was *so* much different than taking my money and investing it into a stock I couldn't see and didn't have control of at the end of the day.

I also want to understand the risks in my investments. How might I lose my money? I remember thinking what would happen if there was a fire, flood, or even tornado that took out my property. However, as I continued to learn, I realized that unlike most other investments, with real estate you have insurance. Fires, floods, tornadoes are covered and in fact I may even come out ahead in a fire or complete teardown. Meanwhile, there is no insurance when the stock market falls 20 percent in a year. In some investments, it's hard to understand the risks due to the sheer amount of information.

DO YOU HAVE CONTROL?

Do you have control over your money? Well, you own the real estate. Unlike with a stock, where you don't own the company but rather a small fraction of the company, with real estate, you actually own the real estate. Therefore you actually have the responsibility and retain the right to make decisions with your money. You have little control and little responsibility with other investments. To me, I want the responsibility and I want the control because I worked hard for my money in the first place. If something goes wrong, I want the ability to correct it or fix those things. Nothing was worse than watching my 401(k) drop and not being able to do anything about it. However, when COVID-19 happened, I didn't just sit there and pray my investments wouldn't be impacted, I had the opportunity to talk with my management company and make changes in real time that allowed my real estate investments to have a fantastic year despite so many obstacles. Having control is VERY important because things like COVID-19 will happen; the world is moving quickly and having the control to adapt with it is critically important.

I liked the answers I was getting early on, but real estate is expensive. *I better know what I'm doing.* I found myself asking, *How much would I even need to buy a property?*

This wasn't hard to find out. Most banks required 20 to 25 percent down. As you become more advanced, you'll find ways to acquire real estate that allows you in some cases to buy it without anything down. I didn't know how to do this right away and you don't either, but it's true and I've acquired many properties with none of my own money.

IS IT PREDICTABLE AND CAN I MAKE THE INVESTMENT MORE PRODUCTIVE?

The short answer is: Yes.

Bear in mind as we go forward that when it comes to real estate investing, I am a cash flow investor, *not* an appreciation investor. That means that I am looking to own and improve properties that I am proud of and that are profitable from day one.

With these three bases covered, we went looking for our first property. Would it be a home run?

THE FIRST INVESTMENT

One thing you will get from most books on real estate is that you should buy in a great location. I didn't know a lot at the time but I did know where a good location was. For my first investment property, I found a single-family house across from a golf course priced at about $75,000. Good location at a good price. Check and check.

For that price, we had to save up about $20,000. It wasn't easy to save up this amount; it took some time. We managed to do so a bit faster due to a promotion and stopping our contributions to our 401(k)s. In keeping with a very high intensity for our vision, we also cut all unneeded expenses.

To mitigate risk we hired an inspector. And it was crazy...I got a full report on everything that was right and everything that was wrong with this investment. I say crazy because with my 401(k) or with stocks, nobody ever gave me a full report that I could understand. Better still, for the things that were wrong, *oh look!*, there was a cost associated with it. Wow, this was pretty cool. I was feeling much more aware than ever about this investment and more than any others before.

What to do next? At this point I could either choose to spend the money to fix what was wrong or I could choose to have the seller agree to fix it. Once again—crazy to me—I had the option to walk away from the investment penalty-free. That option was very big for me because I put a lot of money on the table to be able to get this property under contract. I was still thinking it was very risky, but you know it was nice that I had that inspection contingency. (I recommend this for almost all deals.)

Talk about control, huh? Getting the option to take the investment or to leave the investment. Not like a 401(k) where if you put your money into the investment, it's locked until age fifty-nine and a half, unless you take a significant penalty. No contingency there.

I understand the problems and how to fix them and how much they cost.

Okay, good so far, but it's still a lot of money. What about the returns? This is where we expand on my simple *Yes* to the question, *Is it predictable and can I make it more productive?*

Analyzing the Deal Example: Property Address					
Total Capital Investments:	$ 20,000.00		$ 20,000.00		$ 20,000.00
Purchase Price:	$ 75,000.00		$ 75,000.00		$ 75,000.00
Property Value:	$ 92,896.00		$ 110,180.71		$ 219,009.20
Operating Revenues	**2013**		**2014**		**2021 (Project future yrs.)**
	Monthly	**Yearly**	**Monthly**	**Yearly**	**Monthly**
Average Rents:					
Single-Family Home	$ 900.00	$10,800.00	$ 975.00	$11,700.00	$ 1,485.00	17,820.00
	$ -		$ -		$ -
	$ -		$ -		$ -
	$ -		$ -		$ -
Gross Income (Rents):	$ 900.00	$10,800.00	$ 975.00	11,700.00	$ 1,485.00	$ 17,820.00
Less: (Vacancy/Delinquency):	-3.0% $(27.00)	$ (324.00)	-3.0% $ (29.25)	$ (351.00)	-3.0% $ (44.55)	$ (534.60)
Other Income: (Late Fees)	$ -	$ -	$ -	$ -	$ -	$ -
Other Income: (Utility)	$ -	$ -	$ -	$ -	$ -	$ -
Other Income: (Pet)	$ -	$ -	$ 40.00	$ 480.00	$ 40.00	$ 480.00
Other Income: (Laundry)	$ -	$ -	$ -	$ -	$ -	$ -
Other Income: (Misc.)	$ -	$ -	$ -	$ -	$ -	$ -
Gross Other Income:	$ -	$ -	40.00	$ 480.00	$ 40.00	$ 480.00
Total Gross Rental Income:	**$ 873.00**	**$10,476.00**	**$ 985.75**	**$11,829.00**	**$ 1,480.45**	**$ 17,765.40**
Operating Expenses:					
Real Estate Taxes:	19% $1 66.00	$ 1,992.00	17% $ 168.08	$ 2,017.00	12% $ 179.42	$ 2,153.00
Property Insurance:	3% $ 26.58	$ 319.00	3% $ 27.08	$ 325.00	2% $ 28.33	$ 340.00
Property MGMT:	0% $ -	$ -	8% $ 78.86	$ 946.32	5% $ 74.02	$ 888.27
Utilities:	0% $ -	$ -	0% $ -	$ -	0% $ -	$ -
Maintenance & Repairs:	7% $ 61.11	$ 733.32	7% $ 69.00	$ 828.03	7% $ 103.63	$ 1,243.58
Trash/Snow/Grass Removal:	0% $ -	$ -	0% $ -	$ -	0% $ -	$ -
Total Operating Expenses:	**29% $253.69**	**$ 3,044.32**	**35% $ 343.03**	**$ 4,116.35**	**26% $ 385.40**	**$ 4,624.85**
Net Operating Income:	**71% $619.31**	**$ 7,431.68**	**65% $ 642.72**	**$ 7,712.65**	**74% $1,095.05**	**$ 13,140.55**
Total Debt Service (96K):	39% $ 340.60	$ 4,087.22	35% $ 340.60	$ 4,087.22	23% $ 340.54	$ 4,086.48
Interest on Loan (4.25%):	28% $ 247.10	$ 2,965.22	25% $ 247.10	$ 2,965.22	16% $ 231.28	$ 2,775.38
Principal Reduction (25 AM):	11% $ 93.50	$ 1,122.00	9% $ 93.50	$ 1,122.00	7% $ 109.26	$ 1,311.10
Cash Flow:	32% $278.71	$ 3,344.46	31% $ 302.12	$ 3,625.43	51% $ 754.51	$ 9,054.07
Total Return:	43% $372.21	$ 4,466.46	40% $ 395.62	$ 4,747.43	58% $ 863.76	$ 10,365.17
CF/Debt Service Ratio*:	181.83%		188.70%		321.56%
Cash on Cash ROI:	16.72%		18.13%		45.27%
Total ROI:	22.33%		23.74%		51.83%
Capitalization Rate:	8.00%		7.00%		6.00%

*(125%>)

It was relatively easy after reading a couple of books to forecast the income that the property was going to produce because it was already producing income—somebody was renting it. In the image, that is about $279 per month, or about $3,344 per year. (Throughout the book, we've referred to $3,400 for round numbers.)

It was also straightforward to factor in expenses because there were known expenses: things like property taxes. That's not a guess; you can actually look at what the property taxes currently are or you can look at what the property taxes will be with the new purchase price and the tax rate within the city that you're buying the property. In the image shown, that came out to $166 per month or $1,992 for the first year, 2013.

Before you buy the property, you can ask your insurance agent to give you a quote. So you know exactly what you're going to be paying in insurance. You can estimate utilities. And in this case, my tenants were paying the utilities. So I didn't have any. You could put a percentage of the rent on maintenance repairs. And I learned that you should always estimate maintenance repairs, whether you have some or not. I listed these as 7 percent, or $61 per month. You can estimate after that what the management fee is going to cost for managing it. Even if you manage that property yourself, which I chose to do in this case for the first year, there should be a fee associated with that. Because one day, if you're going to velocitize your money, you might have a manager do this so that you can spend more time finding and funding the next deal. In year two, 2014, I list that as 8 percent, or about $79 per month. Lastly, debt, which is even easier to estimate as your bank will give you that and the best part of the debt is that it is paid by the tenant each month, unlike your home.

After estimating that I realized with the rental income and even with adding some vacancy (3 percent), if that happened, and taking out expenses, I was going to make $3,400 that year (again, rounded up from $3,344 for this example throughout the book). If you would have asked me how much I was going to forecast in my 401(k) in a year, I would have no idea. Would you know? Also, how much in your 401(k), even if you could forecast it, would actually be in your checking account to be able to reinvest? In this case, I forecast $3,400 actually being in my checking account to help me buy my next property. That was $3,400 on a $20,000 initial investment for a 17 percent ConC return. This investment was paying me now, not when I turned sixty. I understood the fees. And at this point in time, while I managed it, I didn't need a financial advisor, so there were no other fees to consider.

As you review the provided image, you can see that in year two, 2014, a few things changed. Rent increased and a pet fee came in to improve income. Expenses increased too, but by a lesser amount, so the net cash flow in year two increased to $302 per month (up from $279 a month) and produced an 18 percent ConC return. By 2021, monthly cash flow was $754 a month producing a 45 percent ConC return.

BENEFITS OF REAL ESTATE

At this point you can already imagine how excited I was to finally get started on an investment that I *understood, could control, and could predict*! But of course, it gets better.

Let's now zoom out a bit from that first investment to take in the landscape of real estate to include a few more critical benefits relative to a common investment: stocks.

CONTINUOUS CASH FLOW

As long as your tenant pays the rent, you have monthly cash flow you can count on. Build in vacancy to accurately predict your annual cash flow on a monthly basis—this lowers risk. If there is some vacancy, you've already accounted for that in your prediction of returns.

Already, this continuity should provide a level of comfort relative to an investment like a company stock for which you have little control: you aren't the CEO of that company, you don't manage that company's operations, and besides stocks that pay a dividend, you generally have to sell a stock position to generate cash flow.

Your ConC return is an annual measure of your earnings on a property compared to the amount you initially spent to buy it and make it operational. The first property I invested in produced $3,400 that year, expressed as a ConC return of 17 percent.

$3,400 came back to me from a $20,000 investment.

Take the return and divide it by investment for that period of time. If we express this annually for that first year, it is $3,400 divided by $20,000, or 17 percent.

The key question is: How fast can you send money out and get it back again to send out again?

The process of answering this question leads to greater and greater velocitation of your money.

Now, this $3,400 changed everything for me. It wasn't a ton of money, but it wasn't about the money. It was rather that it didn't take a ton of *time*. I could accurately understand and forecast my returns and it was easier to understand than I thought. Up until this investment, I tried so many others but none of them answered all my questions. This one did.

ADAPTABLE PRICING

With stocks, the price is whatever the market rate is.

Real estate investment properties are priced based on their profitability. Real estate offers you the chance to take advantage of underpriced or poorly managed properties, whether due to a motivated divorced couple wanting a quick sale or through the previous owner's decision not to invest in that property toward the potential you see in it. The better you can figure out how to make the property more profitable, the more it is worth, especially if the property is five units or more.

REAL ESTATE

For example, on my first property, the expenses were much higher mostly due to the utilities. While the rent was the same, the previous owner paid for all utilities. And when I acquired the property, I had the tenants pay for the utilities. Simply by lowering expenses by 14 percent, that increased my cash flow by 14 percent.

$$\$3,400 \times 1.14 = \$476$$

$476 divided by $20,000 is 2.4 percent more ConC return. While this was not a property that was five units or more, that's an increase in the unit cash flow of $476.

Imagine for a moment this was a building with five or more units, since that tier of real estate properties is priced based on the profit they generate.

In that situation, divide the increased monthly income into the cap rate (the going rate of apartments in this location):

$$\$476 \div 0.06 \ (6 \ cap) = \$8,000$$

With a simple reduction in expenses leading to an increase in cash flow, we have increased the value of the property by just under $8,000 ($476 divided by 0.06). While $476 doesn't seem like a lot, this is one-unit and that $476 a year creates $8,000 of increased value. Now imagine a five-unit or ten-unit. An increase in net cash flow increases the overall value of the real estate investment. We just increased 14 percent on one unit. Increasing that for five, ten, or one hundred units would have a substantial impact on your overall ability to scale and the value of the property itself. And this was only a small change on the expense side. As you've already read earlier in the book, focusing on income creates much more value than focusing on expenses. Now imagine, if you focus on the amount of income your property can generate, what that will do for the value.

LONGER TIME HORIZON ON THE TRANSACTION

With stocks, you put your bid in through an exchange or a broker and if there is a seller you have a deal. The buy process usually happens the same day if not within a few minutes or less.

Of course, real estate transactions take longer.

That's good because it allows you to do your diligence through an inspection report, appraisal to value the property, and other means. It also helps you to avoid hasty, emotion-based decisions.

With the very first deal I did, I took my time to review the inspection report carefully and I was thankful not to be rushed into anything. I could have backed out and never invested in real estate. Fortunately, after doing our diligence, we went ahead and I got my first taste of real estate investing.

REFINANCING TO TAKE
ADVANTAGE OF LEVERAGE

Many people don't realize the advantage that a real estate investment can have on building wealth quickly versus a stock or traditional investment. One of the biggest advantages I can describe in just one word—leverage.

Here is an easy example:

1. You put $20,000 in stocks or invest $20,000 in your 401(k) this year.
2. You also invest $20,000 in a real estate, which buys you a $100,000 property (20 percent down).

Let's say both assets go up this year by 10 percent.

1. Your $20,000 stock or 401(k) investment is now worth $22,000. Growth of 10 percent, not bad.
2. Now your $20,000 of real estate investment grows to $110,000 ($100,000 × 1.1). Growth of 50 percent: $10,000 divided by your original $20,000 investment!!!

The crazy part about this is that we aren't even factoring in the mortgage pay down for the year from the tenants or the monthly cash flow it's paying you every month after expenses.

Leverage makes the difference.

Of course, it is possible to buy stocks on margin; however, this past year put a lot of new investors in a tough situation when they took on the system, whether through GameStop or other stocks. If you face a margin call after losing in an options play, you have the potential to lose quite a bit.

Meanwhile, leverage in real estate can also be very useful to velocitizing your money, *especially if you are taking a cash flow approach*.

For a brief moment, consider that the asset price approach to real estate got a lot of people in trouble in 2008. They were buying a $250,000 house hoping to sell at $450,000, and some of them did, banking $180,000 after $20,000 in mortgage payments and expenses during the two years—for example—that they owned the house. But what about those people who bought the $250,000 house and saw the value drop to $150,000? Of course, they had to foreclose.

This risk doesn't play out the same way if you are focused on cash flow. A property that dips in asset value, even for a few years, can easily withstand the market downturn because it is *productive*. It is producing cash flow. It has the "coverage" to pay down the monthly debt.

Now, once you reach a certain profitability for a given property, it may be time to refinance. Why? First, to save on taxes. And second, to use the money you pull out to invest in yet another property.

In the case of my first property, the first year it was producing $279 per month, or a little under $3,400 a year. At that level, I could nearly write off all the taxes with depreciation (talk to your CPA) and pay close to no, or no, taxes. But what if the monthly profitability increased to $754 as it did by 2021? At over $9,000 a year for a real estate investment worth $219,000, the profitability would be too high to avoid paying taxes.

But here's where things get interesting. This same real estate investment is probably worth a lot more since it's producing a lot more profit. What if by refinancing that increased value out, you pull $25,000 from that investment and used that $25,000 to buy another property that also produced monthly cash flow of the same original amount, $279? Now, by pulling out $25,000, you increased the debt on the first investment property and now the mortgage expense is $100 more per month. This takes your monthly cash flow down from $754 to $654, right? However, the second investment property produces $279 a month, so now your total cash flow return isn't $654, it is $933 ($654 + $279). Now if you include the fact that the increased mortgage interest is a tax write-off, you also are keeping even more of your money and paying less tax. Lastly, imagine if the second investment property becomes more profitable like the first one did and goes from $279 in monthly cash flow to $754 in monthly cash flow. Do you see where I'm going with this?

When you receive your check on a W-2 job, taxes are taken out first, then you spend what's left on needs like your utilities, mortgage, groceries. In real estate it works the other way around: you subtract all expenses first and then add a depreciation write-off. Then, if there is anything left, you pay taxes on that. Take time to discuss with a CPA that is knowledgeable here and it will blow your mind how little you have to pay in taxes with real estate investments compared to other investments. Most people only pay attention to what they make but it's more important to pay attention to what you "keep."

That's a simple example of the power of leverage in real estate.

Now, to be fair, some people do talk about over-leveraging in real estate. This is a reasonable concern because market dips are real, even if the cycles currently seem difficult to predict. However, when as investors we are focused on owning and operating real estate properties, which have solid cash flows, we don't fall into the trap of being over-leveraged in the same way that an asset-price investor would (investing on appreciation versus cash flow). Always ensure when taking on more debt, you have solid cash flow to cover it. In today's world, debt service coverage ratio (DSCR) is much more important than the loan-to-value ratio (LTV). If these terms are new to you and you are a beginner when it comes to debt, I highly recommend education here. There is plenty of information on over-leveraging out there, so I don't want to spend much time on it here. I'd like you to consider making sure you are not *under*-leveraged as shown in my example above and taking on more debt to offset taxes and move the money to the next investment property. This is where velocity of money gets really fun!

If you take a similar approach to mine, remain diligent on providing properties that (1) you are proud of and (2) are profitable. Don't sacrifice either of those like some investors who believe they should cut expenses to eke out a better monthly cash flow. The opposite is usually better. Spend a bit more to justify charging higher rents. Tenants appreciate good value.

Ultimately, you will see that you can utilize debt to increase ConC return in order to scale. Real estate investing is capital intensive. Once you start growing you can recycle capital. That's what refinancing opens the door to.

HEDGING AGAINST INFLATION

Debt is cheap right now while inflation continues to climb. Inflation should be top of mind when you invest your money as it is a serious player in the devaluing of your money and potentially your investment returns as well. Assets like real estate are a huge hedge against inflation. Let's talk about price inflation, debt debasement, and cash flow enhancement.

Let's start with price inflation.

From an inflation standpoint, a property that is valued at $1 million, with inflation of 10 percent, would then have $1.1

million in value. Think about it like this. If you put down 20 percent, or $200,000, your equity would rise to $300,000 (original $200,000 down plus the $100,000 increase in value). From the perspective of ROI, that's five times on your money. The 10 percent inflation, in other words, is *devaluing the dollar but that increases the value of your asset*. You used other people's money (debt) to purchase the property. That initial $800,000 moves with inflation too. That is now your money. So "price inflation" in real estate is a great hedge and in this example it gives you a 50 percent return when it comes to just inflation. The obvious other benefit you are getting in this example is the power of "leverage" (buying the investment using 80 percent debt).

You can also "force appreciation in real estate" to both control your returns and also control how far you push the 10 percent growth. It's a process called "repositioning" your asset. Simply put, repositioning includes but isn't limited to renovations and capital improvements on a property that improve the net operating income.

Next, debt debasement. It is easy to understand but less understood by most beginner investors. Let's say we have a second property with debt on it at $1 million, and we see 5 percent inflation this time. In inflation-adjusted dollars, that $1 million in debt is actually only $950,000 after a year, then $900,000 in year two, then $850,000 in year three. Rents are rising, prices are rising, everything is rising. But that $1 million in debt goes to $850,000 with no action from you. So, locking in that financing is a huge opportunity as it keeps your biggest expense on the real estate investment the same over the years, or with inflation it actually drops in dollar-adjusted currency. Locking in that financing is a huge opportunity.

Then there is cash flow enhancement. Like I shared above, the biggest expense in real estate is your debt. When you buy a property, put on as much debt safely as you can. Let's say it is locked for five years. That means your biggest expense in real estate is *not* moving along with inflation. Maybe rent growth in five years could be 30 or 40 percent, but your debt stays the same the entire time. Remember when my cash flow went from $3,400 to $9,000 on my first property? This is why!

Price inflation, debt debasement, and cash flow enhancement each represent different ways of hedging against inflation with real estate investments.

EXITING YOUR INVESTMENT

In the case of my first property, not only did I get a ConC return of 17 percent, but the ROI was higher at 25 percent because the tenant—not me—was paying down the principal on the mortgage. You don't get that money now but this can be huge to reap later with selling or refinancing.

Furthermore, there's appreciation on this property. I bought it for $75,000 in 2013. In 2021 the property was reassessed and is now worth $219,000. Even better, now it is cash-flowing over $9,000 a year. That's more than double my original ConC return in year one. My money is working at about 45 percent now and picking up speed each year as the rent climbs higher while the debt and most expenses creep up slower than income.

I don't have to pay taxes on the increase in value from $75,000 to $219,000 unless I sell this golden goose. And even if and when I sell it, there's an option of a 1031 exchange where you roll the profits into another property and keep all the gains tax free. Try doing that with your stocks. With this investment, as I shared above with leverage, I simply kept it and chose to refinance instead of selling—this allowed me to take out more than my original investment, move that into another real estate investment, and still keep this one.

AVOID THESE COMMON MISTAKES

My journey in real estate was not without errors and missteps. Learn from mistakes, integrate them into your approach, and move on.

My first mistake: With the first property, I guessed at the market rent. Just because the previous owner was renting it out for $900 doesn't mean I should put the rent there too. I didn't realize that if I did any sort of market rent analysis, that there was nothing being rented out as cheap as what my investment property was. I just continued to rent it out at the same amount. Looking back, I could have rented that out for a hundred dollars more a month, which would have made me not $3,400, but about $4,600. $1,200 more. The difference on that is a return of 17 percent or a return of 25 percent. That is a major mistake, not understanding market rent when it comes to real estate. Not understanding that you can achieve higher income is something that I had to learn the hard way.

The second thing that I did wrong is I chose to manage it without having any experience fixing things. The washer overflowed and stopped working. I got a call from the tenant and I had no idea what to do. Luckily I searched online for people who could fix a washer and took the five highest-reviewed plumbers. The third person I called said they could go out there and fix it, which he did.

If you can't fix anything like I can't, then you should take the time to develop relationships with people who *can* fix things for you and try to get a prenegotiated price. I didn't take the time to do that. The repair took longer, I paid more, and that delay put undue stress on me and on the tenant.

It's a big deal to ensure that either you or your property management company is equipped to perform on the property. If I hired a good property manager on this first investment, I'm confident that both mistakes would have been avoided.

The next thing is financing. I didn't understand financing *at all*. What happened? I put down *way* too much on this property. The bank was asking for 25 percent. I ended up putting about 27 percent down on the property. I didn't understand at this point, the true value of buying more properties. So for example, as you know, the ConC on this investment is about 17 percent, but the loan I got for it was 4 percent. So why in the heck would I pay more down on the 4 percent when I already knew that it was forecasted at 17 percent? Plus, it wasn't even me paying this amount down, it was the tenants who were paying the mortgage. That is a major mistake. Another thing I had to learn the hard way.

One last thing is to get rid of liability. I put this property in my name versus first creating an LLC with an attorney and putting the property into the LLC's name. The risk of personal liability is not worth it; take risk off the table and put your investment properties into an LLC and use a good attorney to do it the right way.

THE PROMISE OF SCALE AND MY INVESTMENT APPROACH

As you pull equity out of properties and reinvest it, your ConC return will increase and then approach infinity, since that metric is the return of cash divided by the investment. You've seen that is a natural result of my strategy, which is simplified as follows:

STEP 1: ACQUIRE PROPERTY

Acquire property with as little down as possible that still cash-flows to safe margin.

STEP 2: REPOSITION PROPERTY TO BE PROUD AND PROFITABLE

Invest to upgrade properties. Look at how the property is running, then optimize it. Make things look, feel, and even smell better. Continue to invest so you are both proud and profitable. Many investors make the mistake of not investing. I prefer to spend money to make money, because what matters for my strategy is cash flow. Income beats expenses, just as income beats expenses in running your life like a CEO. This is a very complex step that takes a while to learn. However, you can keep it simple. Look over your property, think about what you can do to run it or invest in it differently that would either increase income or decrease future expenses. Both will increase the net income or cash flow from the property and make the property much more valuable.

STEP 3: REFINANCE

Unlike the residential home market, real estate properties are bought and sold not according to comparative homes but based on the cash flow they produce (five or more units typically). Another way to think about this is, imagine there are two properties for which everything is the same except one produces more cash flow—which are you more interested in and therefore which is more valuable?

Once I increase the cash flow of a property, I will have it reappraised and refinanced to pull that money back out tax free. That money can be used to acquire new properties. This way you are ensuring you aren't *under*-leveraged, you get tax benefits, *and* you increase the velocity of your money.

I watch my cash flows much more closely than overall asset prices themselves. If a property's asset value goes down to one dollar, I'll still be okay if I have tenants paying rent, because the cash flows will be there and I'll be able to pay the mortgages.

There are a lot of ways to invest in real estate. Find a strategy that works for you that fits the lifestyle you want to live. I am primarily a buy-and-hold real estate investor who focuses on long-term cash flow from my properties. Nothing that I do is short term.

THE BEGINNING

The crazy part is that the benefits of real estate shared in this chapter are only the beginning few. There are so many more you will learn about as you go along.

Look at my first deal again.

These benefits were for a single-family house. As you will learn and as I learned later in my real estate career, when you buy real estate investments that are five units or more, those real estate properties are now real estate businesses. And it opens a door to many more benefits that I encourage you to look into. So if you thought this one provided a lot of benefits, just wait.

Now, I never dreamed of owning over 1,500 units, but with these kinds of benefits, why would I put my money into anything else? I don't necessarily have any aspirations on unit counts in the future. I just want to keep my money working hard. And the crazy thing is in real estate, the bigger you get, the easier and less risky it becomes. You have banks that want to lend and give you more money because of your experience and your overall portfolio. Having one or two vacancies doesn't hurt you because you have so many units. Delinquency doesn't hurt as much either as your volume increases.

To get started, you don't need to know everything about real estate and you don't need to know even 10 percent of what I shared in this chapter. In fact, I didn't. You just need to know more about this investment vehicle than the others you currently invest in. That's the challenge. While this may be overwhelming and while you still may think this is risky, come back to those questions I invited you to ask—about understanding, control, and predictive cash flow. Can you answer those right now for your current investments?

YOUR PROGRESS REPORT
TOWARD FINANCIAL FREEDOM

1. *Honestly challenge norms and beliefs.* ✔
2. *Decide what Financial Freedom is to you, when you want it, and with what intensity level.* ✔
3. *Define and boot up the systems to run your life like a CEO.* ✔
4. *Light up your scoreboard.* ✔
5. *Become financially literate.* ✔
6. *Learn how to scale.* ✔
7. *Teach your sons and daughters to fish.* ✔
8. *See how I built my real estate business.* ✔

The Three-Step Financial Freedom Process:
1. *Set a vision for your life.* ✔
2. *Through awareness and sacrifice, organize your life to increase cash flow with your time.* ✔
3. *Invest your money in assets that increase your cash flow.* ✔

TAP INTO THE GREATNESS INSIDE OF YOU

Many people I talk to don't believe they can soon get out of the rut in which they find themselves. Worse, some don't believe they can *ever* get out. When I'm speaking with someone about their finances—which I do often—I can usually get an indication in the *first minute* of our conversation as to what their limiting beliefs are.

But for those who do believe there is another way, real estate can be a good choice for investment. But as we've discussed, there are critical steps before choosing or rebalancing your investment vehicles.

Above all, how bad someone wants Financial Freedom probably matters most. Let that settle in...

How bad do you *really* want Financial Freedom? Has that changed throughout your reading of this book? The reason I put that question to you is because it might be the most important factor in you actually getting there. You can't just do the steps outlined in Chapters 2 through 4. If your intensity level in Step One isn't very high, then maybe a 401(k) is okay for you. But if you do have a high intensity level and want Financial Freedom, take it, it's yours. Only you know what you are truly capable of, if you have the courage to let it be expressed in the world. You too are the only person who knows the sacrifices you're willing to make to manifest that potential.

To put it even more bluntly, just because you've read this book doesn't mean you'll reach Financial Freedom. Your hunger matters. Are you hungry? If you are, the good news is you don't need the brain of Elon Musk to do this. You don't need to be super smart. You don't need a college degree. You don't need to be a doctor.

I'm a small-town kid with no financial education and I did it by age thirty.

It's the discipline and the focus that matter in the context of that intensity level that lead you to the earliest possible time frame. Don't be on someone else's timeline. Be on *your* timeline. Do it *your* way. Even as you make sacrifices, you can even have fun with it. When you are questioned by others, you'll have ⹁ calm of your conviction. Your plan and mindset are in place.

Hopefully by reading this book you've been equipped with the background knowledge, inspiration, and concrete steps to get started and get there. Especially sooner than sixty-five. There *is* a path to reach Financial Freedom *sooner* than society, parents, and school told you. I hope you see that. And even though there is a path, no one will hand it to you. Sacrifice and focus are very important. Not just monthly sacrifices in expenses, but sacrifices in **how you spend your time.** You can watch show after show on Netflix or you can read a book. You can put off your freedom or you can do something about it. You don't have to be amazingly smart to understand money; you just need to be prepared to think differently from how you're programmed to think.

I'm confident that *anyone* can do this. Take your vision and your detailed timeline. Then, if you reflect on your last thirty days, recognize and change the behaviors on the next thirty days, combined with awareness of how you're spending and investing, combined with education on how money can work hard for you too, and apply hunger, discipline, and focus, following the rest of the ideas in this book, I'm very confident that you'll reach Financial Freedom faster.

If you are honest with yourself, you'll get excited about the hard work ahead. Few things worthwhile are gained easily. Self-reliance and personal responsibility and simply making the *commitment* to take charge of your financial decisions changes you right here, right now. What's the alternative?

Getting organized in terms of money, investments, and finances is crucial to reclaiming control of your life. Too many people have given away control for too long. Including me. Including you. It's time to step out of the darkness and into the light.

Put aside fear. Consider the story about my totaled car. You might say that a fear of change held me back from an important insight about money. But eventually I became frustrated again, and my manager said, "Read a book!" I am thankful for that wake-up call and others along the way.

If you set aside resistance and work on something different every day, you can do that. Especially if it's difficult, that pursuit will be rewarding.

You can learn to run your life like a CEO. The systems you develop and fine-tune will only improve with time. The process that you use is as important as those near-term goals.

I've given you a few tools to give you a head start:

- How to set a vision, including determining your intensity level
- How to build awareness by focusing on cash flow monthly
- How to make your assets and liabilities more productive, that is returning cash to you faster, which can be

invested yet again for maximum velocity through passive monthly cash flow

Use these. They are powerful.

Setting a vision matters because it not only sets an aim for the adventure of your life but also allows you to make the case (to yourself!) for the time horizon and manner in which you go on that journey.

Then you build awareness. Start tracking your earned income and investment income. Subtract your expenses and you have your monthly net cash flow. Over time, how can you flip the script to increase the ratio of investment income to earned income?

With discipline and focus, your increasing cash flow allows you to apply the results of your financial education to make investment decisions that increase the *productivity* of your net worth, not simply your net worth total alone. First bench bad investments, then cut them, and finally invest only in your top-performing investments. I've shown you the door. Will you take it? Whether or not you choose real estate as your primary investment vehicle, following the above steps will put you in a position to scale and truly benefit from the rebirth of options in your life.

When you've begun your journey toward Financial Freedom, please drop me a line to share how you're doing. Better yet, when nearly there, send me an email—logan@loganrankin. com. I want to know how you did it. I want to know how you feel. I bet you'll be feeling pretty darn good.

There's only one way to find out. It's time to set aside fears and society's expectations. It's time to chart your own course. It's time to tap into the greatness within you and take the leap into the adventure of your life.

ABOUT THE AUTHOR

Logan Rankin is an experienced and strategic entrepreneur who quickly achieved financial freedom after starting with nothing except personal drive and a desire to fulfill his potential. Having built two multimillion-dollar businesses and owning more than $150 million in real estate by thirty-four, Logan spent the first decade of his career working with a Fortune 50 corporation, leading retail operations. He formed a reputation for building high-performing teams, managing large P&L portfolios, and implementing strategic operational changes at the enterprise level. He lives in Wisconsin with his wife and two children.

To continue to follow my journey and receive more financial literacy content, visit www.loganrankin.com or by following me on social media channels.

Made in the USA
Monee, IL
11 May 2022